RESPONSIBILITY BEYOND GROWTH

A Case for Responsible Stagnation

Stevienna de Saille

Fabien Medvecky

Michiel van Oudheusden

Kevin Albertson

Effie Amanatidou

Timothy Birabi

Mario Pansera

With a foreword by Richard Owen

BRISTOL
UNIVERSITY
PRESS

First published in Great Britain in 2020 by

Bristol University Press
University of Bristol
1-9 Old Park Hill
Bristol
BS2 8BB
UK
t: +44 (0)117 954 5940
pp-info@bristol.ac.uk
www.bristoluniversitypress.co.uk

British Library Cataloguing in Publication Data
A catalogue record for this book is available from the British Library.

ISBN 978-1-5292-0817-7 hardcover
ISBN 978-1-5292-0836-8 ePub
ISBN 978-1-5292-0835-1 ePdf

Cover design: blu inc, Bristol
Cover image: Alberte Oro Claro/Mani Moretón
Printed and bound in Great Britain by CPI Group (UK) Ltd, Croydon, CR0 4YY.
Bristol University Press uses environmentally responsible print partners.

FSC
www.fsc.org
MIX
Paper from
responsible sources
FSC® C013604

Contents

List of Figures and Tables

Figure

Tables

About the Authors

Kevin Albertson (Irish/New Zealand) is Professor of Economics at Manchester Metropolitan University. His recent work considers the economic impacts of climate climate change, public policy analysis, and the ways, means and implications of public sector commissioning in the areas of social policy and criminal justice. Kevin's writing has appeared on blog sites such as the Conversation, and he has participated over a period of years in radio and televised discussions of topics ranging from, for example, governments' budgets and autumn statements to the behavioural economic guide to Christmas. He is a co-author of the Haynes Manual *How to Run the Country* and other books including *Payment by Results and Social Impact Bonds: Outcome-Based Payment Systems in the UK and US*; *Justice with Reason*; *Justice Reinvestment: Can the Criminal Justice System Deliver More for Less?* and *Crime and Economics: An Introduction.*

Effie Amanatidou (Greek) is Honorary Senior Research Fellow at Manchester Institute of Innovation Research at the Alliance Manchester Business School, University of Manchester. She studied Maths at the Aristotle University of Thessaloniki (Greece) and holds an MSc in Technical Change and Industrial Strategy and a PhD in Foresight Evaluation from the Manchester Institute of Innovation Research. Effie has over 20 years of experience in research and innovation policy analysis including in particular foresight studies and evaluation/impact assessment of research and innovation policies and programmes. Since 2014 Effie has taken up a special interest in social innovation especially in relation to grass-roots initiatives emerging in contexts of financial crises in the South of Europe. Her interest in this area has been focussing on developing a typology of social innovation in relation to other innovation types and examining its 'position' in the research and innovation systems and the consequent policy implications.

Timothy Birabi (Nigerian) is currently a corporate strategy consultant in London. He has a PhD in Economics from the University of Glasgow where he worked as teaching and research staff for four years. His research at Glasgow mostly focussed on applied social statistics and empirical econometrics. At University of Sheffield, he was an ESRC-funded research associate exploring the spatial dynamics of ethnic inequality in the Glasgow housing market and in the regional development of Hebei Province, China. Tim's current research interests mostly focus on economic value modelling and in understanding the systemic limitations of comprising units within aggregated social, political and economic structures in the quest for growth/progress.

Stevienna de Saille (American/British) is Research Fellow in the Institute for the Study of the Human (iHuman) at the University of Sheffield. She has an MA in Gender Studies and received her PhD in Sociology from the University of Leeds in 2013, studying feminist knowledge production at the emergence of reproductive and genetic technologies in the 1980s. Subsequently, she was a Postdoctoral Research Fellow on the Leverhulme Trust Research Programme, *Making Science Public*, focussing on 'The Emergence of Responsible Research and Innovation'. At iHuman, she works on responsible innovation in the fields of genetics and robots for health and social care. Stevienna is a founder of the Fourth Quadrant Research Network on Responsible Stagnation (4QRN), and was a member of the Strategic Advisory Group in the formation of the UK Association for Studies in Innovation, Science and Technology (AsSIST-UK). She is also on the Advisory Panel for the journal *Science as Culture*, and was for four years a co-convenor of the Science and Technology Studies Study Group of the British Sociological Association.

Fabien Medvecky (French/Australian) is Senior Lecturer in Science Communication at the University of Otago. Fabien has a PhD in Philosophy from the University of Sydney and PGDip in Economics and works on the role of values in the interaction between science and society, focussing predominantly on the way ethics and economics are engaged in social decisions around science. His current research focuses on the ethical and justice issues in the way scientific and technological knowledge is made with and communicated to the public. Fabien has published on ethics, economics, ecology, science communication and science policy and is the current president of the Science Communicators' Association of New Zealand.

Mario Pansera (Italian) is Assistant Professor in Innovation Management at the Universitat Autonoma de Barcelona in Spain. He gained a PhD in Management from the University of Exeter Business School in the United Kingdom. His dissertation focussed on the discourses of innovation and development with a particular interest for the Global South. His primary research interests are Responsible Research and Innovation, sustainable and ecological transition and the critique of the development discourse and growth. He is also particularly interested in the dynamics of innovation in emerging economies, appropriate technologies, and grass-roots and social innovations.

Michiel van Oudheusden (Belgian) researches how science, technology and innovation (STI) are governed in diverse sociotechnical fields, including new and emerging technologies and nuclear science and engineering. From 2008 to 2012, he reflected with Flemish nanoscientists and technologists on how nanotechnologies shape new, collective futures for his PhD thesis at the University of Antwerp on the politics of participation in technology assessment. While based at the University of Liège (from 2012 to 2015), he compared Flemish and Walloon STI policies. In 2015, he joined the Belgian Nuclear Research Centre SCK-CEN, where he studied safety and security governance, citizen-driven radiation monitoring, and reached out to policy makers, scientists, members of civil society, and the public at large, with a view towards inciting Responsible Research and

Innovation in the nuclear field. He is presently employed as a Marie Skłodowska-Curie research fellow at the University of Cambridge (from 2019 to 2021), where he researches and facilitates interactions between grass-roots citizen science groups and formal institutions, such as public authorities and research communities. He is a cofounder and coordinator of the FWO-funded Belgian Science, Technology and Society network (B.STS) and a lecturer at the University of Liège.

Additional Contributors

Keren Naa Abeka Arthur (Ghanaian) is Lecturer at the Centre for Entrepreneurship and Small Enterprise Development (CESED) at the University of Cape Coast, Ghana. She holds a PhD and an MBA in Entrepreneurship and Innovation from the University of Exeter Business School, UK. Her work is multidisciplinary and includes studies on the responsible emergence of financial innovation, entrepreneurship education and training in religious institutions, gender and enterprise development and sustainable business practices within SMEs in Ghana.

George Gritzas (Greek) is Assistant Professor at the School of Spatial Planning and Development, in Aristotle University of Thessaloniki (AUTH) and a founding member of the academic board of the post-graduate program "Social and Solidarity Economy" at the Hellenic Open University. Currently (2020) he is leading a grant for the study of the relationship of networking with social economy and social innovation, and is also part of a research team studying models and policies for affordable housing in Thessaloniki, Greece.

Andrea Jimenez (Peruvian) is Lecturer at the University of Sheffield's Information School. She holds a Msc in the oxymoron that is sustainable development, with a specialism in information and communication technologies for development (ICT4D) and a PhD at the School of Management at Royal Holloway University of London. She is presently exploring the concept of *Buen Vivir* (*Sumak Kawsay*), an indigenous Latin American intercultural approach, and exploring the theoretical implications of changing the lens on innovation to a *Buen Vivir* Approach.

Poonam Pandey (Indian) is Research Fellow at the Department of Science and Technology-Centre for Policy Research (DST-CPR), Indian Institute of Science Bangalore. She holds a Ph.D. in Science Policy from Jawaharlal Nehru University, New Delhi. For the past eight years, she has worked on the intersection of STS, innovation studies and development studies. Currently, she is looking at the value trails in innovation in order to understand how values are created, promoted, circulated and imposed through the ideas and practices of innovation.

Foreword

Richard Owen

It was Hannah Arendt who once famously said that most evil is done by those who never make up their minds to be good or evil. In the Richard IIIs, Edmunds, Iagos and Don Johns we can readily recognize malice and intent. Indeed, they may even tell us they want 'to prove a villain'. Arendt is talking about a different kind of villain: those who do not think, those who do not reflect on the meaning or consequences of their actions, or inactions. Those who choose not to choose.

Innovation can be defined in many ways, but for me the key thing is that it is about creating futures, in sometimes profound and disruptive ways. Innovation is a powerful thing, but it also has the propensity to be tragically banal. Think about all its promise, potential and power and then think about what it is actually being used for. At a time of great danger for our planet and the people and non-people who inhabit it, think about the futures innovation could create, and the ones innovation is actually creating. We desperately need innovation to help us secure a future on this planet that is sustainable, flourishing, just and equitable, but that is not what we are getting. Not all innovation, to be sure. But a great deal, and that is the sad truth.

With innovation I suggest the time has come to choose to choose. What kind of futures do we want (or rather need), and want innovation to help create? How can we collectively and substantively engage with those futures? And what does that mean for the re-framing and practice of innovation now? These for me are the departure points for taking responsibility for the future and for responsible innovation.

Responsible innovation, or at least the version I am familiar with, has always been cognisant and critical about the economic and political contexts within which it sits (I won't go on about second order reflexivity here, other than to stress its importance). This is a book that goes further. After reflecting on this context, the authors have made a choice. They contend that innovation is trapped in its 'feed-the-market' ties as the engine of an unsustainable, growth-led economic order. They suggest instead a framing of innovation that is driven by responsibility with a specific normative orientation: agnostic about growth, aimed at restraint, moderation, ecological sustainability, empathy, collaboration, and slower, ethical decision-making.

Now I am not sure 'responsible stagnation' (RS) is ever going to catch on. But that is what this book is proposing, and, given the fact that we can't go on as we are, whatever we call it, it's important. There will be those who recognize cognates and antecedents: whether it's the slow food movement in Italy, 'lagom' in Sweden or 'sumak kawsay' in South America. There are a growing number of people out there who think in similar ways, the future is not determined or decided.

Like many interesting initial ideas, those in this book are not fully formed. That is to be expected, and will need a little patience at times on your behalf as the reader. So it is perhaps the concept of time that I will leave you with here. This is a book which stresses slowing down, making more careful and measured decisions, taking time to reflect on the things that matter and where we really need to channel our innovative capacities. I agree with that, but I also have a sense of urgency if we are to have a flourishing and sustainable future on this fragile planet. Time is not on our side. We urgently need innovation to do some hard work for us. But it is innovation of a particular kind, and we need to make choices. Sometimes innovation may feel trapped in a system where there is little option for change. But not always. And at those precious moments where we have some agency, those moments when we can choose to choose, this book provides some clues as to what choices we can make.

Preface

When we first began discussing the concept of 'responsible stagnation' (RS), the possibility of this referring to a voluntary near-total shutdown of economic activity never entered into anyone's mind. Yet as we go to press, whole countries, as well as individual towns, cities, states and provinces across the world are doing just that in the hope of controlling the spread of a novel coronavirus, COVID-19.

We are aware that the world in which we wrote this book may differ in many aspects from the one in which it will be read. Yet when we ourselves stagnated production in order to reconsider the text, we found that very little of what we had written needed to be changed. This is not because we foresaw a crisis coming, but because the systems and assumptions we discuss are still informing policy decisions, even as the most responsible choice – preserving life over preserving the economic status quo – is thankfully being made. What will happen as we exit the present crisis is impossible to predict from where we currently sit, with close to four billion people under some kind of confinement. We do not know what the innovation landscape will look like when we finally exit from our locked-down state, or the kind of work 'innovation' will be asked to do. The only thing we can state with certainty is that the COVID-19 pandemic has already catalysed an astounding wave of invention and innovation – in its broadest sense – and will continue to do so for some time.

The book you hold is an outgrowth of discussions which took place between the founding members of the Fourth Quadrant Research Network on Responsible Stagnation (4QRN) between 2017 and 2019. Of that larger group, seven of us (de Saille, Medvecky, van Oudheusden, Albertson, Amanatidou, Birabi and Pansera) undertook the actual writing down of some of the ideas developed through a series of virtual seminars and honed during face-to-face workshops and conference panels. Although each chapter is credited to a particular author (and in some instances, their collaborators from other projects), all seven of us have contributed throughout. Thus, the book represents a range of aspects which we think sit together conceptually and narratively to make this more than a collection on a theme, and we have worked hard to make it a coherent whole. Yet because we come from different disciplines, from sociology to economics to politics to philosophy, the voice and tone of each chapter may also differ. This is intentional. It reflects the variety of authorship, our backgrounds, and our interests.

Not only do we come from a variety of disciplines, but also from a variety of worldviews. We do not necessarily all agree with all the views expressed in the various chapters. Sometimes we might disagree with individual claims, sometimes with broader arguments, and sometimes we might hold almost conflicting views/ideals. Still, we all find value in the variety of views expressed because this is part of what we see as an urgently needed and ongoing discussion; it is part of the multiplicity we see as a necessary aspect of RS. As a group, we were not aiming to develop a consensus, but rather to learn from each other by bringing attention to what we each see as useful, rich and important at the intersection between innovation and the real economy.

The entire book, therefore, is to be read as the result of the network's sometimes uneasy combined knowledge, as one continuous argument about the kind of work 'innovation' is being made to do in the real economy and how we might improve its effect on existing social and planetary systems. It is not a choral piece sung harmoniously with a well-structured melody guided by a conductor; rather it is something more like jazz, with all its sometimes discordant improvisations and off-track pursuits, yet there is still an underlying rhythm and theme to which we continue to return. We invite you to tap your feet along with us.

The Fourth Quadrant Research Network
April 2020

Acknowledgements

Collectively, the authors would like to thank the other members of the Fourth Quadrant Research Network on Responsible Stagnation (4QRN) for their ideas, inspiration and encouragement as we began to draft this book. Particular thanks go to Douglas Robinson, Daan Schuurbiers, Tsalling Swierstra and Pablo Herrera for the long discussions at the very start, and to our friends, families and colleagues – with special honours to Erik Fisher, David Guston, Paul Martin, Catrinel Turcanu and Ine van Hoyweghan – for their ongoing and very patient support.

We would also like to thank the Independent Social Research Foundation (ISRF), who supported the formation of 4QRN with a Small Groups Grant in 2017–18, enabling us to establish the online seminars and two face-to-face workshops from which this book emerged; the editorial team at Bristol University Press, particularly Paul Stevens, who was not put off by a book with seven authors talking about stagnation; the anonymous reviewers whose insightful comments sharpened our argument profoundly; and of course, Richard Owen, who keeps us thinking.

Stevienna de Saille's work on Responsible Research and Innovation (RRI) has been supported by the Leverhulme Trust under Grant RP2011-SP-013, and in part by the National Science Foundation under Grant SES-1343126.

Michiel van Oudheusden's work has been supported by the European Commission's Horizon 2020 MSCA-IF-2018 research funding scheme, under grant no. 836989.

Portions of this book were previously published as: de Saille and Medvecky (2016) 'Innovation for a Steady State: A Case for Responsible Stagnation', *Economics and Society*, 45(1), pp.1-23 (available Open Access).

The 'responsible innovation matrix' is adapted from Guston, D.H. (2015) 'Responsible innovation: who could be against that?' *Journal of Responsible Innovation*, 2(1), 1–4. Used with permission. Join the discussion at http://fourthquadrant.org.

PART I

Welcome to the Matrix

The neoclassical (Solow-Swan) model of growth suggests that material technologies and innovations are required to increase social progress. Acknowledging that innovations often have uneven impact, responsible innovation (RI) was originally conceived as a way of negotiating acceptable risk and shaping innovation towards filling real social needs rather than merely increasing profit and national Gross Domestic Product (GDP). However, the embedding of RI into science funding policies, particularly as Responsible Research and Innovation (RRI) in the European Union's Horizon 2020, has increasingly been used to strengthen the same growth paradigm it was meant to challenge.

Drawing on insights from ecological and steady-state economics, and from science and technology studies (STS), we question how the growth paradigm shapes and limits the innovation space, and consider how innovation can facilitate progress in a more environmentally and socially responsible manner.

1

Introducing Responsible Stagnation as the 'Fourth Quadrant'

Stevienna de Saille

In the still-smouldering aftermath of the global economic meltdown of 2008, Former World Bank economist Joseph Stiglitz (2009) predicted that capitalist economic systems would now need to enact profound change. As of 2019, the political answer still appeared to be that, as Margaret Thatcher so staunchly insisted back in the 1980s, There is No Alternative. Capitalist systems had largely returned to business as usual. Around the world, the rich got richer while inequalities grew, wages stagnated, and a war on public services was waged under the flags of 'austerity' and paying down national debts. Yet post-industrial countries continued to experience relatively low levels of growth in comparison to the pre-crisis years, at least as measured by Gross Domestic Product (GDP).[1] Policy makers made status-quo choices in the belief that to do otherwise was to risk a return to the disastrous stagflation of the 1970s. Thus, accelerating innovation – in the sense of getting more new things to the market faster – increasingly became championed as not just a good way, but The Only Way to stimulate economic growth. And then, early in 2020, a novel coronavirus appeared, demanding a policy response that at first appeared unthinkable: to shut down as much of the global economy as possible in order to slow the progress of the virus as it spread around the world.

Where the global economy is right now is not where it was when we wrote this book, and it is far too early to tell where it will go. It is entirely possible that once the health crisis recedes, the same rhetoric will re-emerge – that *only* (market-based) innovation will allow us to navigate the economic crisis which will inevitably follow. We do not argue that for-market innovation will have no role to play in how our economies recover, nor can we try to predict how the shutdown is likely to affect our innovation systems. With the number of countries issuing stay-home orders still rising as we go to press, that would be both premature and beyond what we originally set out to do. Instead, we hope to broaden the conceptual landscape within which decisions will be made by not losing sight of where we were when this latest crisis began, what assumptions have been made about the relationship between innovation and growth, and what options (and constraints) were already in the system – and still are. Therefore, we begin by asking what is 'innovation'? And how has it become the be-all and end-all driver of economic growth, as if there were no other form of economic activity, no other way to produce what we need to live good lives? How much growth is really desirable, and of what kind, when ever larger sections of the population in historically richer nations are benefiting less and less from increases to GDP, while the environment and its biodiversity suffers more and more from the economic activity we already have?

Alternatives are clearly needed – not only to growth, but to the models, assumptions and discussions that limit our ability to challenge the doctrine that there is no other way to fulfil our needs and aspirations. Yet, despite the evidence of the last decade, the intertwined claims that free markets provide the optimal incentive structure for innovation, that innovation drives economic growth and that economic growth is necessary for human progress, have remained exceedingly difficult to disentangle. Clinging to this belief has meant that the state's primary function seems to have been reduced to enabling market-based growth which can be measured by GDP, rather than safeguarding precious resources and seeking ways to spread the fruits of innovation to all its citizens to improve the overall quality of national life. Politicians too often champion measures which enable short-term growth regardless of long-term outcome, such as lowering corporate taxes (which reduces the prosperity of the state) and freezing wages or curtailing labour bargaining rights (which reduces the prosperity of citizens), thus in fact *increasing* economic stagnation (as those without money cannot buy what is produced), which in turn requires even more desperate measures to increase GDP. In other words, as Tim Jackson (2018) and others have argued, the increasing social and environmental breakdown we have been witnessing since 2008 is not caused by lack of growth itself, but rather by the pursuit of growth at any cost.

Despite all this – or perhaps because of it – there have been innovations even within this GDP-obsessed system which have not necessarily seen growth as a primary goal. These include social enterprises, benefit corporations and novel means of sharing and recirculating goods or bartering services. While they may indeed still contribute to GDP, these innovations are aimed at creating and/or more equitably dispersing *prosperity* – loosely defined as a state in which one's basic needs are met and there are ample opportunities for creating meaning in one's life, whatever that might entail. In other words, unlike innovation for GDP growth, innovation for prosperity can take place outside the market as well as within it, increasing prosperity in ways that GDP is not designed to measure.[2]

Along with a number of other rising voices, this leads us to ask: what is the economy *for*? Is it simply just to grow? Even Simon Kuznets, creator of the Gross National Product (GNP)[3] statistic, argued in an oft-quoted statement that there were important distinctions between quantitative and qualitative growth, that 'goals for "more" growth should specify more growth of what and for what' (1962, p 29). Is it to improve the quality of life? Traditional economic models are based on the theory that 'rational' humans invariably act to maximize their own benefit, but this would not necessarily improve society as a whole (indeed, maximizing one's own benefit generally comes at the expense of others). As Quiggin (2010) has put it, 20th-century economic models based on rational actor theory may be internally consistent, but they have also been consistently wrong. Humans are intensely social beings who do not have perfect information, and the coronavirus pandemic clearly shows that we can make decisions based on ethics, altruism or the common good, as well as fear, greed, ideology and lies.

This book is not intended to be a definitive conversation on this topic, but it does represent a useful start. It is meant as a resource for entrepreneurs, policy makers, administrators, civil society organizations, academics, activists – in short, anyone who seeks innovative solutions to specific global challenges, but who is also concerned about the impact of policies which seek growth for the sake of growth. In the chapters that follow, we will examine some alternatives, and hence, set out an alternative interpretation of innovation and stagnation than is normally found in such discussions. In so doing, we are as indebted to ideas which have long been circulating, such as steady-state economics (Daly, 1991 [1977]), as we are to post-crisis reimaginings such as the 'doughnut' between social foundations and the ecological ceiling (Raworth, 2017), the strength of more equal societies (Wilkinson and Pickett, 2009), the distinction between prosperity and growth (Jackson, 2009), the case for 'enough' (Dietz and O'Neill, 2013) and the need for science and technology (S&T) policies which promote new forms of what is termed 'responsible' innovation (Owen et al, 2012; von Schomberg, 2013). While we begin from the same neoclassical models normally taught in graduate economics programmes, we also draw from what is commonly called 'heterodox' economics – a range of theories which generally have in common an understanding that humans do not always act rationally or in their own best interests; that history and culture are an important determinant of economic systems; that these are not fixed and stable but are by nature complex, unpredictable and evolutionary; that intangibles such as values and power have observable and malleable effects; and above all that there is no singular, infallible theory or ironclad set of rules which can explain or solve every problem.[4]

In other words, we are not setting out to reinvent the wheel. Rather, we are pointing out that as it is presently discussed, the innovation cart is lurching around on only three wheels and we are seeking to draw attention to the fourth, which has been sitting unnoticed by the side of the road all along.

The background to our story

We begin by examining the very term 'innovation', which to economists, most policy makers and the business community denotes new or improved goods and services entering the market, or a new process for providing existing goods and services more cheaply. However, its definition in general speech is looser, simply meaning something new which is taken up and circulated by others – whether inside, outside or even against the market. Freecycle, for example, created the idea and infrastructure for an international online network of local groups which give still-usable items to other members for free rather than selling or throwing them away, as a deliberately anti-market innovation aimed at providing for people's needs while reducing consumption and waste.[5]

The very concept of 'innovation' is therefore also subject to innovation (de Saille, 2015). The last few years have seen the development, largely among academics and policy makers, of a concept of 'responsible innovation' (RI). Although the details may differ, in general RI suggests that innovation should be aligned to social needs, responsive to unfolding ethical, social and environmental impacts as a research programme develops, and include the public as well as more traditionally defined stakeholders such as industry and civil society organizations in two-way processes of consultation, beginning long before a new technology would reach the market and continuing to evaluate its effects once it does (see Stilgoe et al, 2013; Sutcliffe, 2011; von Schomberg, 2013). In 2012, some of these discussions were codified by the European Commission (EC) Directorate-General for Research and Innovation into a new policy framework, 'Responsible Research and Innovation' (RRI), which promised to promote innovation in accordance with European social values. RRI was represented through six 'keys' which aligned with the broader goals of the Lisbon treaty: ethics, better governance of technology, gender equality, open access to scientific information, science education and public engagement (EC, 2012). However, this was embedded within the Horizon 2020 research programme (which allocated European research funding from 2014 to 2020), which was in turn embedded within a flagship policy called Innovation Union (EC, 2010a) aimed at increasing GDP-measured growth. Thus, 'innovation for growth' became not only the rallying cry of science, technology and innovation (STI) policy in the EU (and elsewhere), but has ultimately become a goal in and of itself (EC, 2010b).

This assumption that innovation must and will deliver growth now shapes much of the actual deployment of RI, despite its various frameworks, which stress reflection and engagement (henceforth, we will use RRI when specifically referring to the EU's framework and RI when speaking more generally). The narrow definition of 'first used in a company's production process or is first offered for sale' (Swann, 2009, p 23) explicitly links 'innovation' with the creation of monetary value, as does the demand for new technology to reduce labour costs. Both help to explain the coupling of innovation – as if there were not many other forms of productive economic activity – with GDP growth. Investing public money into innovation is meant to stimulate growth by making the country (whichever country) more competitive, but the emphasis on innovation-for-growth has also closed off many of the arguments about responsibility as stewardship, care-taking for the future, and more equal distribution of risks and benefits with which discussion of RI began.[6]

Additionally, while RI has directed much attention to the need for greater inclusion of the public in the development of new technology, considerably less attention has been paid to the differing understandings of the word 'innovation' among the multiplicity of actors now engaging with various aspects of RI, many of whom have a more expansive definition of that word. RI has often been described as being set in a matrix of binary opposites (responsibility versus irresponsibility; stagnation versus growth), so that agreeing innovation is desirable can effectively black-box questions about the desirability, let alone feasibility, of continual growth. In the following sections we offer a deeper examination of how these underlying assumptions reinforce the GDP-growth paradigm, and consider what might happen if we look more carefully at the meanings of both innovation and stagnation.

Stagnation, innovation, responsibility and growth

One of the underlying assumptions of STI policy is derived from the Solow–Swan model of long-run economic growth. Taken as the starting point for most neoclassical models, it presents growth as resulting from three inputs: capital accumulation, increased labour and technological progress (productivity). Technological progress is not explicitly linked to social progress in this model (although it often is in other discussions), but is defined simply as *any change that leads either to an increase in the levels of output for the same levels of input, or a decrease in input for the same levels of output* (Hubbard et al, 2012). The Solow–Swan model points out that past a certain point, called the productivity peak, achieving growth through more labour results in diminishing returns over time. In other words, increasing the workforce population will increase output, but also increases labour costs. In the absence of technological progress, the result will be a 'steady state' where capital is still produced, but is largely offset by production costs and depreciation, and thus there is no growth.

As measured by growth in GDP, it would appear that most developed economies have reached this point – a prolonged, possibly even permanent, state of slow growth, which the American economist Larry Summers (2013) refers to as 'secular stagnation'. Hence, innovation – particularly 'disruptive' innovation which creates a sea-change in production processes or entirely new sectors – is seen as not just desirable, but the only way to re-establish growth. Unfortunately, disruptive innovation also invites unforeseen consequences – the global financial crisis being a case in point, having its basis in rapid economic growth produced through innovative investment instruments which no one understood.

Exactly what this means in the broader sense of innovation as the take-up and circulation-of-novelty is not clear. In order to make sense of what we mean by responsible stagnation (RS), we must first make sense of the matrix of responsible innovation (Figure 1.1).[7] As Figure 1.1 illustrates, stagnation is generally understood as the antithesis of innovation. Thus, if innovation is a positively loaded term, then – as the model is binary – stagnation can only be used in a negative way. The more innovation is seen as the driver of growth, the more likely any slowdown in the activity of *getting new things to the market* (not in economic activity per se, as that can encompass many kinds of exchange) will be equated with the threat of economic stagnation (Blauwhof, 2012). However, as we noted earlier, much depends upon exactly how one defines innovation. It does not seem possible that humans – an intensely curious and inventive species – would ever stop innovating in terms of creating new objects and new ways of doing and knowing things, and sharing this with others. So, if we define innovation as simply bringing something novel into the public sphere (whether for the purpose of creating monetary value or not), then stagnation is improbable, and 'responsible stagnation' is a vacuous term. It is only by restricting 'innovation' to the market that 'stagnation' takes on meaning as a credible threat.

Figure 1.1: The responsible innovation matrix

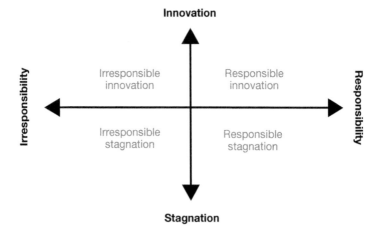

This distinction between innovation as circulation-of-novelty and innovation as bringing-to-market is of crucial importance. For example, Innovation Union is aimed at generating 3 per cent annual increases in GDP across the EU, and RRI is embedded in that policy structure. This would suggest that, in order to be responsible, innovation must contribute to GDP. The perverse corollary would be that innovation which displays all the other desirable qualities of RRI – sustainability, stewardship, public engagement and equally distributed societal benefit – but in fact reduces throughput and therefore reduces GDP, becomes de facto irresponsible according to the matrix. Further, GDP discounts the claims that future generations might have on exhaustible resources, such as the world's ecology or biodiversity, because growth also demands increased energy, which is often a hidden cost, particularly in service innovation. New companies which store data in the cloud, for example, may create an ecological benefit by reducing paper consumption, but will incur a much higher environmental cost through the building and maintenance of server farms and the energy required to run them.

In other words, as the matrix in Figure 1.1 illustrates, if stagnation is understood to be the antithesis of innovation, these become linked together in such a way that not to innovate is *invariably* to stagnate, with all the negative associations that implies. But if we define innovation as 'the process by which novelty is taken up and circulated in the public sphere ... producing some kind of profound re-ordering of what-has-been' (de Saille and Medvecky, 2016, p 7), does the lack of *market-based* innovation truly lead everything to grind to a halt? Could the fourth quadrant of the matrix, 'responsible stagnation', be an equally important part of innovating responsibly, and if so, what might that entail? As Guston (2015, p 2) notes in his own discussion of the concept of RS, there is a central paradox here which is worth exploration:

> Given that innovation in part is what got us into this mess of pushing past planetary limits in an unsustainable fashion, and that the drive for growth and the satisfaction of the human needs and desires of a still increasing human population globally is what compels innovation, we need to consider how we can stop being dependent upon innovation and growth to get what we want ... [But that] is

going to be dependent upon on the generation and implementation of new knowledge and social and technological innovation each step of the way.

In other words, while stagnating *irresponsibly* (as developed economies appear to be doing) may indeed be leading us to our own destruction, *responsible* stagnation does not have to mean a cessation of invention, novelty and creative problem-solving. The matrix shows us four quadrants, two of which are irresponsible, which we of course wish to avoid. But concentrating only on the quadrant for responsible innovation leaves out the potential for innovating in ways that help us manage 'stagnation' responsibly, whether this is by exploring the possibilities of steady-state economics, or by engaging in the deliberate, carefully managed elimination of technologies, sectors and activities which are increasing, rather than ameliorating, the problems we face.

We see this 'Fourth Quadrant' as being complementary to RI, as enabling us to fully utilize all the possibilities of the responsible side of the matrix, regardless of the effect on GDP. Throughout this book, we intend to show that even in its purely economic definition, stagnation is not necessarily the outcome of lack of innovation. Economies can stagnate for reasons other than new things not coming to the market (the old things presumably still being available) and 'innovation' has historically not had the emphasis as 'the driver of growth' that it has recently come to acquire. In this sense, innovation is something which occurs both within and outside the market, and stagnation – in the secular sense of slowing down – may, in some cases, be desirable, even necessary, as it has been in the response to COVID-19. Daly (1991, p 17), for example, considers the steady state as optimal, 'an economy with constant stocks of people and artefacts, maintained at some desired, sufficient levels'. This is not a state of stagflation in which productivity slows while prices continue to rise, but rather a continuing re-balancing of overall productivity across the entire economy (as innovation and external events will still cause different sectors to rise and fall) so that we produce what we need, but not more for the sake of more.

The problem we face is not only that innovation is expected to contribute to GDP, but that GDP measures only economic throughput, not economic health. It does not, for example, distinguish between entire populations purchasing improved nutrition and one multi-millionaire purchasing a new yacht, or between building new housing and rebuilding after a brushfire. In terms of GDP, the more people who buy drugs to cope with depression and anxiety about the future, the better. Coupled with profit incentives, the drive towards growth through faster, more disruptive innovation, come what may, is a huge enabler of activities on the irresponsible side of the matrix, and poses the greatest roadblock to RI itself, which requires time to think and deliberate, rather than simply rush to market with the next new thing. Technologies can fail or produce unexpected problems, markets can dry up, and society itself is not always receptive to the changes scientists, entrepreneurs and policy makers hope to create. At the same time, good innovations which could produce real benefit are too often set aside for others which produce greater or more immediate financial returns.

The impetus towards 'responsible' innovation has its roots in these dilemmas, and so frames responsibility as finding ways to make the trajectory of research and development (R&D) activities more socially beneficial as well as more environmentally sustainable, particularly with regard to technologies whose risks are irreversible and hard to predict. This is the other paradox which appears as RI becomes operationalized through STI policy in various countries, and poses a real challenge for the increasing numbers of willing entrepreneurs who want to create ethically and environmentally responsible businesses and business models: how does one innovate responsibly in a system which incentivizes *irresponsible* behaviour as being 'more competitive'? To answer such questions, we must look beyond economics to better understand how technological innovation interacts with the other elements of society.

Technological progress beyond 'productivity'

As we will discuss further in Chapter 2, in addition to assumptions about innovation and stagnation, there also tends to be an assumption that technological progress should always be pursued, regardless of potential negative outcomes, that it is, in fact, inevitable. The argument here is that technology is inherently neutral, and what makes it good or bad is how we decide to use it. However, the contribution of science and technology studies (STS) scholars over the last thirty-odd years suggests otherwise. As a field of knowledge, STS attempts to unravel, and in some cases improve, the relationship between science, technology and society by understanding how these *co-produce* (that is, exert a mutual influence upon) each other. STS argues that technology is neither inevitable nor neutral. The reality is much more complex – we bring into existence technologies which allow us to pursue our goals, and in turn our societies (and our sciences) are shaped by the technologies available to us and the meanings we attach to them. This profound interweaving of STI with the norms and values of the social world creates fundamentally important questions about the role of science in society (and the role of society in science), how knowledge is produced and validated, what research is funded and which technologies attract investment, and about how contemporary knowledge-driven economies are to manage the strategic, moral and other uncertainties that innovation can produce.

In other words, unlike the policy models which show innovation proceeding on a straight path from the laboratory to the market, STS shows us that innovation is not really linear and easily guided; it is complex, multidirectional, and its effects are extremely difficult to predict. Technological innovation in the late-modern era does not simply happen. It can be a product of scientific research, but it is also a result of political decision-making, accompanied (we might even say driven) by less tangible processes – for example, social trends, novel forms of expertise and ways of organizing research, lobbying activities, public controversies over S&T issues, and a new national government's growth objectives. Jasanoff and Kim (2009) have referred to this as the 'sociotechnical imaginary', a publicly shared, actionable combination of values, capacities and aspirations which guide technological development towards a particular goal. There are reasons, for example, why money has been poured into developing hydraulic fracking as a new technology for extracting fossil fuels in some countries, while others are investing similar amounts towards funding improvements in the storage and generation capacities of wind and solar. These have as much to do with the public's perception of the environment as having intrinsic value, as a particular government's political configuration or economic goals.

Examining how societies shape technology and vice versa troubles the idea of neutrality, by pointing out the many decisions it takes to bring a technology into being, from the initial idea, to funding and carrying out the research, to how it becomes embedded in the market; decisions which are never neutral. There is always a purpose, guided by values which have enormous power to direct which technologies are developed and which are not. However, these values can change, or be contested by different cultures, social identities and generations. Capitalist logics of growth, accumulation and markets are also not singular – there are many flavours and varieties of capitalism which combine with other social values to shape different attitudes towards social progress and technology, and create different political economies of innovation.

It is because of this complexity that this book is a collaboration between economists, STS, development and political scholars. We see growth as a value shared by many entrepreneurs, scientists, policy makers and citizens, but it is not a physical law. It is a social agreement, just as money itself is a social agreement to accord a specific exchange value to paper and metal stamped with certain configurations.[8] As long as the agreement holds, the possession of money in an agreed form confers real-world power. When it fails, as for example with the Deutschmark at the end of World War II, a wheelbarrow full will not buy a loaf of bread. Such values may be powerful, but they are not set in stone.

Similarly, there is a social agreement that growth will lead to social progress, but this depends on what is measured and how. Growing disparities between economic models and lived reality is causing that social agreement to be questioned, even by those who believe in general that market-based capitalism represents the best chance for human progress. This brings us back to Kuznet's stress on the difference between quality and quantity of growth. Before the global shutdown, we had often heard that job growth was strong, meaning unemployment in many developed economies was at an all-time low if the quantitative figures for numbers of people applying for unemployment benefits were used. Qualitatively, however, more and more of these jobs were insecure and/or fell into the category of self-employment within the gig economy, multiplying the economic effect of the health crisis as people's income disappeared overnight. Even without such catastrophic events, it remains true that despite increases to national GDP, wage growth has been largely stagnant for years. In real terms, this means most people are working more to earn less in terms of being able to pay their basic bills, and companies are turning profits of billions which are not being put back into the economy through either increased wages or increased tax contributions. Since the 2008 financial crisis, growth has too often been about new millionaires being able to buy new yachts, rather than millions of hourly workers being able to buy better food.

A number of prominent economists are now arguing that over-valuing GDP-measured growth in economies past their productivity peak has led to a hollowing out of society, [9] so that increasing GDP in richer nations no longer guarantees improvement to the average person's quality of life (see Stiglitz et al, 2010, among others). However, if we stop valuing growth as an *objective* (although it may still be an outcome), our concept of innovation opens up, as does our understanding of whether it helps or undermines social progress. STS allows us to see technology, innovation and the political economy as values-based and co-produced, and therefore more amenable to change than we might realize.

But can we really talk seriously about *stagnation*?

Even accepting for the purpose of this particular argument a definition of innovation as 'only that which is for the market', we would still argue that under normal circumstances *economic* stagnation, with all its accompanying imagery of a fetid, decomposing swamp, is not really possible, although there can certainly be stagnation of growth as measured by GDP. As Schumpeter (1942) has argued, capitalism is constantly in a state of creative destruction, growing and shrinking simultaneously as new technology makes processes, workers and material objects obsolete, and new sectors emerge. Adding nothing new to the market does not mean nothing new is added to society, or that economic activity (a term which can also include non-monetized exchanges of goods and services) would not grow outside the formal market in innovative ways, as it did, for example, in Greece during the Euro crisis. However, let us be clear that we are also not arguing *for* that kind of stagnation of market-based innovation.

What we *are* arguing for is an understanding of innovation as co-produced: it does not stand apart from the research system, the political economy and the society in which it is embedded, nor can its 'success' be defined purely by sales figures, stock prices or contribution to GDP. Instead, we want to ask three important questions: 1) How do we innovate responsibly in secularly stagnant economies without destroying the environment and our social welfare in the process? 2) Is it possible to instead take an a-growth (van den Bergh, 2011) approach to innovation, to aim this at reducing input rather than increasing output, at mitigating the processes of creative destruction by acting with care, and taking seriously the need to reduce the kinds of economic activities which destroy cultures, environments, opportunities and futures? 3) Under what circumstances might this constitute not the opposite of RI, but a crucial and neglected part of the responsible innovation matrix?

First, to reiterate: when we talk of RS as an a-growth approach to innovation, this does not mean that there will be no new things entering the market. An RS approach can still stimulate socio-economic growth, although this may or may not be reflected in measures of throughput such as GDP. However, RS also enables RI to look beyond that which is destined for the market. It allows us to return to 'responsibility' as a moral goal of stewardship for the future, and ask, along with some of the early proponents of RI, if 'any process of responsible innovation that simply serves to target innovation at those "right impacts" which support and compound an increasingly dysfunctional, and unsustainable Capitalist socio-economic world order [could] be viewed as an irresponsible innovation in itself?' (Owen et al, 2012, p 755).

Second, predicting exactly how an RS approach would affect the economy is exceedingly complex. The effects would depend on how much non-market-oriented innovation was still occurring, as well as how much for-market activity was being displaced. Freecycle, community clothes exchanges and repair cafes, for example, could stand accused of contributing to stagnation within the retail economy, as they encourage people to recirculate and repair existing goods for free rather than purchase something new. As niche activities, they do not presently affect GDP in any significant way, but if similar practices of local exchange, gift and barter were to be taken up widely and supported as part of the economy within a national population – in the same way that, for example, recycling has been in some countries – this might not remain the case. As such, socially beneficial RS might indeed reduce GDP, but would contribute enormously to increasing social and planetary wellbeing. More important, it might also help to create a new social agreement, one that directs innovation at ways to re-use what we already have (which, in fact, often does contribute to GDP, for example, through new processes for ragging unsalvageable textiles to make insulation which is then sold).

We see RS, therefore, not as a policy framework, but rather as an intellectual space, the Fourth Quadrant of the matrix, where we can explore the ways in which innovation (broadly defined) may be done more responsibly. It includes, but is not limited to, RI concepts such as engaging the public in determining the trajectory of research and innovation, and using anticipation and reflexivity to consider the most socially and environmentally responsible pathway towards a specific goal. Rather than a roadmap or a set of rules, RS refers to **a particular configuration of change**, one that emphasizes a position in which **ethics matters** as an axis of decision-making in policy, in economic activities, in the social shaping of technology, and in regulation of the market. It is not a particular kind of ethics in and of itself, but rather a way of approaching innovation that does not brush ethical questions aside to focus purely on the technical (as is so often the case in regulatory or consultative mechanisms which claim to be open to the public), and does not allow monetary value generated to outweigh other values-based concerns. Rather, RS calls for integrating a techno-scientifically accurate analysis into ethical and social discussions, just as it calls for meaningful incorporation of questions about collective social and environmental benefit and/or harm into techno-scientific research agendas, roadmaps and industrial strategies. If it advocates any particular ethical approach to innovation it is one of **restraint**, of not disrupting merely for the sake of being disruptive or seeking growth for the sake of growth, but of seeking innovation in the broadest possible sense to find new ways of **living gently** upon the earth and with each other. It is both a response to a profoundly unstable period of human history, and an initiator of **new ideas which consider the scope and pace of change** to be part of innovating responsibly.

In Part II of this book, we will delve deeper into questions about broadening governance to better include the public in decision-making, particularly in the area of publicly funded scientific research and innovation (Chapter 2) and how this is influenced by the economics of responsibility, markets and growth (Chapter 3). In Part III, we will look more closely at stagnation itself, and how responsibility may be reimagined in this context (Chapter 4), introducing real-world examples which take a similar a-growth approach to filling social needs (Chapter 5). We then expand to a more global view, considering locally specific forms of innovation in the Global South, and how RI/RS may support environmental sustainability, social justice and human progress across the world without repeating the patterns of colonization (Chapter 6). Finally, we consider the specific challenges facing willing firms when trying to innovate responsibly within the existing economic system (Chapter 7), before concluding with a final discussion of the scope of RS and how it might change RI itself (Chapter 8).

We should conclude with the thought that RS does not claim to have *the* answer. Rather, we see it as a set of questions which can and should be asked as an integral part of discussions about RI − not in opposition to it. It is, to boldly mix metaphors, the fourth wheel which needs to be reattached rather than reinvented, and without which the cart can do little more than turn in circles, going nowhere very fast.

PART II

What's Wrong with Innovation and Growth?

A sensible question, but one whose answers are more complicated than many realize. Here, we first set out the meanings attached to the concept of innovation and ask how it has recently come to occupy the political and economic position it now holds. In particular, we draw from science and technology studies (STS), which has long sought to better incorporate the public into science and technology decision-making, and from which some of the impetus towards connecting 'responsibility' with 'innovation' derives. We then explain how initiatives towards better inclusion of citizens in decision-making have informed the European Union's framework for Responsible Research and Innovation (RRI), and what is missing from this approach in terms of understanding the place of innovation and its politics in the present political economy.

Continuing directly from this, we will consider the problems which arise from reliance on markets, exploring why the 'optimal solutions' they are supposed to offer have often turned out not to be so optimal after all. Here we lay out the economic foundation of the book in language accessible to the non-academic, introducing concepts such as the Prisoners' Dilemma, explaining what Gross Domestic Product (GDP) actually measures and considering why this does not provide an adequate determination of societal health.

2

Challenges to the Story of Innovation

Michiel van Oudheusden

The connection between innovation and economic growth is not new. For more than two decades, policy professionals and economists of various stripes have promoted innovation as a major source of economic and social development, arguing that it is a must for the creation of well-paying jobs, securing social welfare and strengthening capacities for international competition and global growth. The Organisation for Economic Co-operation and Development (OECD) claims that innovation is both a 'proven driver of sustainable growth' and 'imperative', especially in a time of slow economic development, global warming and rising prices for natural resources (OECD, 2015). Accordingly, OECD member states – mainly high-income, knowledge-based economies – promote the rapid development of new technologies, products and services, as well as industrial renewal and transformation to make their economies more productive and competitive. For example, in a 2008 government-sanctioned report entitled *Innovative Flanders: Innovation Policies for the 21st Century*, we read that Flanders must ensure 'innovation-led growth' (NRC, 2008, p 31), as the welfare and wellbeing of the Flemish people depends on high-tech innovation in the wake of globalization. The report emphasizes that Flanders must invest in science and technology (S&T) so as to maintain its position as a leading innovation region (NRC, 2008, pp 14–32).

The equation of a region's or country's wealth with its innovative capacity is not spurious – Flanders is overall wealthier than Wallonia, the French-speaking area of Belgium. The Nordic countries and others which invest over 3 per cent of their Gross Domestic Product (GDP) in research and development (R&D) tend also to have a higher quality of life, often accompanied by strong social welfare systems (and the higher taxes which support them). It seems obvious that funds raised from the public through taxation and reinvested in the public through research grants, start-up funding and other incentives will contribute to job creation. This, in turn, increases the general circulation of goods and services, all of which is reflected in GDP even if no new goods or services ever make it to the market as a result. Therefore, as we will discuss further in Chapter 7, it is not innovation per se which stimulates growth, but *investment* (without which, of course, most market-directed innovation would not happen). Richer countries with more of a tax base from which to invest will continue to grow richer as long as state investment continues, as the private sector alone cannot create this beneficial upward spiral. This presents a key difficulty for countries which have little overall to spend on research, as the only other obvious entry point to wealth creation is to offer low corporate taxes, lax regulation and an educated but comparatively low-paid work force – a strategy which does indeed create jobs and growth, but does not necessarily spread wealth throughout the population.

Thus 'innovation' is being made to do more work than just bringing new things to the market. It also helps shape a particular investment climate, and is in turn shaped by the political economy in which it is being deployed. Particularly during austerity programmes in which the state reduces its investment in society overall, it becomes imperative to convince the public that investment in the research and innovation system (as opposed to housing or social welfare) has legitimate benefits. For example, to increase this legitimacy (and as a response to what at that point was an ongoing crisis in the Eurozone) the lead-up to the launch of the EU's Framework Programme for Research and Innovation, Horizon 2020, included reshaping the priorities of the earlier Framework Programmes into 'Grand Societal Challenges', so that climate change, energy, food, security, transport, health and ageing were re-framed as threats to the very survival of our species which could only be addressed through an intensification of innovation (for example, see EC, 2010). This enabled an increasingly singular emphasis on innovation as the solution to Europe's economic and social problems, which was coupled with other longstanding initiatives aimed at involving the public more meaningfully in the governance of both the EU and S&T policy, to emerge as the 'six keys' of Responsible Research and Innovation (RRI). In this chapter, we explore how this particular interpretation of responsible innovation (RI) evolved from programmes for public understanding of science and engagement activities often led by science and technology studies (STS) scholars, how RRI has travelled since and what is missing from this approach.

Science and society in the innovation matrix

The dynamic interaction between science and society has profound, often paradoxical, implications. Although expertise is still sought after, it is also increasingly vulnerable to being challenged from different perspectives, which in turn undermines the authority of experts. The politicization of scientific expertise, for instance through cherry-picking or selective choosing and sharing of evidence, has meant that just as we have more need for experts to help us understand where S&T is taking us, we trust them less.

Levidow (1998) argues that in the 1990s, policy debates were *scientized,* particularly in the area of new and emerging technologies, such as agricultural biotechnology. As the debates centred on safety, science education and risk communication, technical experts assumed a high level of political authority and, wittingly or unwittingly, narrowed the regulatory domain to matters that could be adjudicated on the basis of scientific information alone. In this way it became extremely hard for non-experts to engage in debate with experts, as the dominant discourse was technical and scientific rather than ethical or social. To give another example, in most countries before a dam, bridge or other large-scale infrastructure project is initiated, natural scientists and technical experts study and predict the potential impacts such constructions have on the environment through so-called Environmental Impact Assessments (EIAs). Project proposals that do not undergo an EIA are not considered for public (or private) funding. However, assessments are often limited to issues such as pollution, animal habitat and related issues, rather than allowing discussion of, for example, the value a forest may have as an unspoiled place to enjoy nature. Consequently, actors that speak a non-technical language have considerably less public credibility (Gismondi, 1997). It need hardly be said that some innovations – for example, those employed by the agro-industrial complex – are not necessarily in the interest of society at large. This separation of technical and social allows them to fulfil the limited conditions required for operation, leaving the public few options outside of protest to draw attention to any other issues.

Arguably, more subtle forms of scientization can also be distinguished, which are more about using the authority of science to identify problems for the purposes of creating new markets. The philosopher and historian Michel Foucault speaks of the medicalization of insanity (1972), by which he means that emotions and traits are turned into treatable conditions and cures are sold. Shyness, for example, has now become Social Anxiety Disorder, while restless or very energetic children are labelled with Attention Deficit Hyperactivity Disorder, creating lucrative new markets for medical innovation.

Thus, modern-day S&T develop in a context where society at large is encouraged to have high expectations of benefit, but where 'facts are uncertain, values in dispute, stakes high, and decisions urgent' (Funtowicz and Ravetz, 1993, p 735), and where, we might add, incentives are often unclear. This is unquestionably the case with new and emerging sciences and technologies, such as fracking or genetic editing, where local and global investments in R&D are considerable and strategic uncertainty is high, and where people tend to have concerns about how the technology will be deployed. Confronted with many unknowns, including a lack of procedures and social institutions to regulate technology development, policy makers, natural and social scientists and industry representatives increasingly call for the 'democratization' of expertise as a means of handling the complex, unpredictable and disorderly interplay between science and society (Rogers, 2008). These calls for an effective and more accountable technology governance form the background against which the EU's RRI framework emerged.

The paradox of scientific innovation is this: science might dictate what *can* be done, but not what *should* be done. For instance, new sciences like oncology and epidemiology give rise to contradictory knowledge claims, which scientists are not yet able to untangle. Yet, without scientific evidence, we are in no place to judge how to proceed. A further complication is that the funding structures in which scientific research is embedded increasingly demand proof of 'impact', generally by yielding patents and marketable products. This is particularly true of emerging fields such as nanotechnology, biotechnology and robotics, which are expected to have socially significant outcomes, but are primarily expected to make a significant contribution to national aspirations for competitiveness and economic growth.

Participation and public engagement with science

Increased scientific complexity and strategic uncertainty, as well as public ambivalence about S&T, means that we have been searching for new modes of organizing science that are better attuned to the needs and values of society for some time. As scientists increasingly confront one another, for instance in debates over what constitutes real versus fictitious environmental impacts of technology or the benefits and dangers of nuclear power, there have been calls for a more participatory science, one which broadens the spectrum of actors and perspectives in technological decision-making. Since the 1960s, such demands for broad public engagement in science have intensified, as new social and civil rights movements challenged ineffectual governance by technocratic elites, and organizations such as Science for the People[1] emerged with the aim of democratizing

S&T culture. Today, the scientific process itself has become an issue of public contention and debate, resulting in disputes over what constitutes relevant knowledge, and casting doubt not only on the possibility of value-free science but the validity of facts and evidence in decision-making.

What emerges instead among various publics is scepticism, even a profound distrust, of science based on the argument that its activities are deeply politicized and marketized, and that actors and institutions interpret, craft and explain the facts in accordance with their views and interests in the adoption of a given technology.

To counter this loss of legitimacy, renowned public institutions are now echoing what were once radical demands for society-wide science participation. The UK Royal Society, for example, explicitly calls for the involvement of wider society in science, with the aim of helping to decide 'how technologies develop and where research and development effort is focussed' (Royal Society, 2019). Echoing the European Commission's RRI Framework, such programs underscore the need to build capacities for socially inclusive R&D by developing innovative ways of connecting science to society (EC, 2019a). Arguably, they reflect a broader institutional shift away from a linear conception of innovation (for example, Science *and* Society programmes) towards notions that embed science in society (for example, Horizon 2020's Science *with and for* Society). These new orientations unfold with new policy forms of dialogue in S&T, including citizens' juries, public dialogues, and stakeholder engagement, which are in turn structured around the idea of aiming innovation at 'Grand Societal Challenges', such as climate change or clean energy – defined as problems which are global in scope and solutions from which all people can therefore expect to benefit. Participation is expected to foster collaborative governance and produce innovation outcomes that meet everyone's needs. It builds on tried and tested governance approaches, such as Technology Assessment (TA), and aligns with contemporary approaches of organizing science, such as Open Innovation, for the sake of achieving both economic development and social wellbeing (EC, 2016).

Yet, it is not clear whether participation in S&T governance can actually meet these aims. In institutionally organized participation formats, such as stakeholder dialogues and consensus conferences, the grounds for favouring public participation are often to avoid negative social impact of new technologies, or to build public confidence in decision-making. When this is the case, dialogue and engagement are valued primarily for their instrumental potential, that is, in view of realizing particular predefined ends, such as social stability and public trust (Stirling, 2008). This framing limits opportunities for democratic debate about the means and ends of technology development by excluding voices that are critical of established scientists and their institutions. It also comes with a considerable risk – that public engagement and participation in science will merely serve to facilitate the innovation-for-GDP-growth paradigm, rather than opening up wider social and political questions about purposes, ownership, power and responsibility, such as: who benefits from this technology and who bears the risks? What is needed to make this technology work? Can we imagine viable alternatives? (Macnaghten et al, 2005). Accepting the partiality and inevitable uncertainty of scientific knowledge (that is, that science itself can change as new discoveries are made) and that it is a good (but not the only) means of producing knowledge, points to the need for science to be scrutinized by all potentially affected parties, including a plurality of publics (Saltelli et al, 2016). These publics deserve to have a say in decisions which affect them personally, and a need to develop publicly reasoned quality criteria for science which consider political, ethical and social concerns as intertwined with technical ones.

From innovation to innovation governance

Although no single description of RRI exists and the RRI concept is continuously evolving, René von Schomberg (2011), who works for the European Commission on research and innovation policy, offers the following widely accepted definition:

> Responsible Research and Innovation (RRI) is a transparent, interactive process by which societal actors and innovators become mutually responsive to

> each other with a view to the (ethical) acceptability, sustainability and societal desirability of the innovation process and its marketable products (in order to allow a proper embedding of scientific and technological advances in our society). (von Schomberg, 2011)

In this formulation RRI is best understood as an interactive process that actively solicits society's informed opinion about innovation processes. The idea is to bring about a certain configuration of change, that is, to render innovation more ethically acceptable, sustainable and democratic by ensuring that non-technical concerns are also integrated into innovation processes at an early stage, rather than as an afterthought or a response to rejection. To this end, RRI is envisioned as a key part of the research and innovation landscape, to be established as 'a collective, inclusive and system-wide approach' involving all stakeholders, from policy makers to civil society organizations to scientists and citizens (Sutcliffe, 2011, pp 55–6). As it invites reflection both on the products and purposes of science and innovation, it denotes an orientation towards anticipation, inclusiveness, responsiveness and reflexivity concerning S&T and innovation processes more broadly (Owen et al, 2012; Fisher and Rip, 2013). Ultimately, the definition of RRI requires us to ask a key question not previously addressed: *to whom* (not just for what) is innovation responsible? It is in this area that the concept represents its own innovation on prior formulations of assessment such as TA, which only assess what an innovation might do technologically, in the narrow context of its deployment. For example, TA can assess a fracking technology in terms of groundwater and air pollution, potential for earthquakes and noise disturbance, all of which impact on the people living nearby, but cannot incorporate impact on the value of properties in the area or the systemic effect of prolonging the use of fossil fuels. RRI is meant to incorporate these wider impacts, as well as the idea that responsibilities can change and are often in simultaneous and intractable conflict – for example, between residents and county councils who do not want fracking in their area (or anywhere) and the government and specific fracking companies (and their shareholders) who do.

As RRI is a policy innovation in-the-making, it includes many agendas and stakeholders, and its boundaries are continuously being negotiated and redrawn. As attested by various authors and by RRI practitioners,[2] its meaning remains elusive, even though it mandates the 'opening up' of science and science policy processes to society and bears strong similarities to other contemporary science policy approaches, such as Constructive Technology Assessment and Anticipatory Governance. Furthermore, RRI may also include forms of corporate social responsibility, social innovations and system innovations that exceed and extend the context of science- and technology-driven research and innovation. For instance, EU-funded RRI projects cover a wide range of topics, from reducing overconsumption, adapting to climate change, and managing challenges faced by start-up businesses, to supporting new forms of science education, and research into the function of gender in science beyond how many women work in the lab (RRI Tools Consortium, 2016, p 15).

All of this is welcome, but we see it as insufficient, particularly as it still seems to consider questions about the political economy in which research and innovation is carried out to be outside its remit, despite the focus on 'society'. Although RRI is intended as an open-ended experiment in 'innovation governance' at large, which engages multiple actors, stakes, processes and outcomes (Felt et al, 2007), it is, as with von Schomberg's definition, generally aimed at stimulating market-driven innovation for the purpose of GDP-measured growth. As de Saille (2015, p 161) has noted elsewhere, this may explain some of the tensions presently inherent in RRI as a policy framework. To begin with, although Owen and colleagues (2012, p 752) referred to an 'emerging zeitgeist' across the European political arena that a new kind of STI policy was needed to safeguard both the environment and the public interest against economic demands, subsequent policy documents have largely framed RRI as a way that public resistance can be avoided and market success ensured (for example, see EC, 2013):

> In effect, the documents show alternately a research-oriented weighting towards ideas of democratic deliberative processes, ecological stewardship and

specific problem-solving (although this has also been critiqued as a technological fix for the problems technology has created), and an innovation-oriented weighting towards 'grand challenges' as opportunities for creating, expanding and exploiting new markets. (de Saille, 2015, p 159)

RRI proponents also typically frame interaction between scientists and wider society as an inherently transparent, inclusive deliberation rather than as a process that involves the strategic use of power and influence (van Oudheusden, 2014). This framing conceals how RRI is coloured by a deliberative-consensual view of democracy and political legitimacy that encourages open dialogue among relatively small groups of participants about specific issues, such as gender equality in science and research ethics. What is missing in this perspective are broader political and economic considerations, such as how growth imperatives may exacerbate or even cause gender imbalances, for instance by penalizing women who have family responsibilities, and questions about how responsibility in different innovation systems gets apportioned and distributed. Even if we accept that social dialogue occurs under favourable circumstances and that it can effectively lead to better policies and better policymaking, it still remains to be seen how the outcomes of deliberation can be made to count in real-world science and policy arenas when growth is the ultimate goal. Numerous political studies indicate that power elites (that is, policy makers) are disinclined to cede formal power to citizens, as these elites owe their position to representative constituencies whose opinions may differ (Lövbrand et al, 2011). Furthermore, innovation cycles are largely determined by research industry players (big technology firms, pharmaceutical companies, food multinational companies and others), who to this day are only rarely or remotely included in RRI processes.

These observations raise critical questions about the scope and utility of RRI in contemporary knowledge-based economies. Although RRI challenges the orthodox understanding of innovation as a linear process from basic science to applied research and production, and although it proposes to take into account societal and ethical considerations, it also continues to promote the idea that innovation is the driver of growth *and* social wellbeing (Blok and Lemmens, 2015, p 19, emphasis added). We iterate that the second is not a given, nor is there a causative relation between the two – the discrepancy between GDP growth and concurrent stagnation of wages in real terms in many countries over the last three decades being a primary case in point.

Under this innovation-for-growth approach it is also unlikely that RRI will effectively and decisively re-orient STI towards meeting pressing societal challenges and towards engaging with the real needs of broader segments of society. To render R&D, businesses and regulatory practices more socially and environmentally sustainable, a more critical engagement with RRI is needed, one that not only asks what constitutes 'responsibility' in innovation, but also considers how dominant notions of responsibility accord with broader techno-political agendas, and explores the possibilities for cultural change and political economy reform. We may, for instance, choose to acknowledge the limits to economic growth rather than ignore them at our peril, question the unstated normative aspirations and motivations that underpin science and innovation, and place more emphasis on issues of power, trust and relationships (both historical and new) in innovation processes. As we will argue in the next chapter, RRI/RI alone cannot provide the antidote to the dominant growth-based innovation paradigm, partly because its focus on the market inhibits its capacity to fulfil its ideals. We also need to look beyond the European and Eurocentric views of RRI presented in this chapter, and to explore the many different approaches to more responsible forms of innovation that emanate from elsewhere, particularly outside the market (Chapter 5) and in the Global South (Chapter 6).

3

The Problem with Markets

Kevin Albertson

In his 2004 book, *The Company of Strangers*, the economist Paul Seabright recounts an anecdote of his time spent advising leaders of the former USSR on the adoption of market economy. In response to the perplexity of a Russian official who asked, 'Who is in charge of the supply of bread to the population of London?' Seabright responds, 'Nobody is in charge' (Seabright, 2004, p 10). This is, of course, the power of the market system. It delivers outcomes without the need for central planning – there is, however, no guarantee that all outcomes delivered by the market will be socially desirable.

Supposing the official had asked, 'Who is responsible for climate change and the impending mass extinction of many of the Earth's most vulnerable species?' The answer would have remained 'nobody' – mass extinction being one of the unfortunate side effects of the market system (Wright and Nyberg, 2015). A solution may exist – let us hope it does – but it will not be a free-market solution. It might even be a solution in which markets are constrained to produce rather less harmful outcomes. Indeed, this is what we argue later in this chapter.

Similarly, just as the tiny self-interested actions we all choose in a free-market context amount to ecological disaster on a global scale, so the tiny decisions we all make in a free-market context can amount to economic disaster on a global scale, as happened from 2007 to 2008. For the global financial crisis, no one is solely responsible; rather it was the globalized free-market system emphasizing growth while evading responsibility which inevitably gave rise to such an unwanted side-effect.[1] In this chapter, we critique two of the central concepts of the current political-economic system: the ill-considered adoption of market-based policies and the general fascination with headline economic growth (GDP) as a worthwhile policy objective.

As we have previously argued, the problems which arise from reliance on markets are often disguised by the definition of 'progress' as economic growth. We would not want the reader to conclude, however, that we believe there is no role for markets – far from it. Our argument is rather that markets (and growth) ought to serve society, rather than vice versa. Our criticism of markets essentially consists of the observation that the conditions under which they give rise to an optimal solution are not often met. Indeed, by continually exacerbating inequality, for example, socio-political paradigms based on the free market contain within themselves the seeds of their own destruction.

There are those who suggest, as Adam Smith (1812, p 318) would have it, 'They [the rich] are led by an invisible hand to make nearly the same distribution of the necessaries of life, which would have been made, had the earth been divided into equal portions among all its inhabitants.' This 'invisible hand' hypothesis suggests human interactions, societies and even civilizations can most easily be built, not in a planned or deliberate fashion, but rather by rational individuals' pursuit of their own self-interest (Seabright, 2004). Indeed, it has been suggested that any attempt to shape this process, through, for example, democratic governments' regulation of the market to improve social outcomes, will rather more hinder than help such progress (Friedman, 1962). This point of view has provided a theoretical foundation for those who promote a doctrine of deregulated market-based political-economic policy to facilitate such pursuit. Friedman and Friedman (1980, p 247), for example, suggested 'the free market system distributes the fruits of economic progress among all people'. History, however, indicates the benefits of the market will accrue to those who wield the greatest power. As Friedrich Nietzsche (1908, p 112) has pointed out, 'Justice is … reprisal and exchange upon the basis of an approximate equality of power'. Where power is unequal, reprisal and exchange might not be 'just' – or efficient. Thus the invisible hand of the market may rather become the invisible fist of those who control the market.

As an example, we might consider how the poor, by definition those with the least market power, pay higher prices or endure lower quality (Andreyeva et al, 2008) for many goods and services compared to the affluent. Some examples might be rent-to-buy contracts where the total amount is significantly more than the item would cost if paid for in one go, pre-paid energy schemes which charge a higher per-kilowatt hour price than is charged to accounts paid by direct debit, and high-interest payday lenders. In short, those who earn the least often pay the most in order to subsist. We might also note that the already wealthy will have a greater proportion of their income after subsistence available to invest and thus are more able to increase their future wealth and income relative to the poor. Those lacking market power, on average, pay more today and will earn less tomorrow than those enjoying market power. The market, it would seem, reinforces inequalities rather than efficiently distributing the fruits of economic progress.

Turning from the individual to the collective, we might consider the concentrating power of the market and its effect on businesses. Because of economies of scale, large businesses are generally more efficient than small or medium enterprises (SMEs) and/or more able to buy out (and hence close) their competitors. Added to this, we might also consider that those with economic power can influence the rules of the market to their own favour (Cave and Rowell, 2014) through, for example, monopoly power, corporate lobbying to influence policy and large donations to politicians who may thus be incentivized to serve their interests. It follows that, over time, even minor inequalities in people's and firms' market power will become accentuated and that inequality will increase. This is what is known as the 'Matthew Effect', which is best summarized by the adage that, over time, 'the rich get richer and the poor get poorer' (Merton, 1968). It has been speculated that only cataclysmic events (that is, market-breaking events) – mass mobilization warfare, transformative revolution, famine, state failure and lethal pandemics – reverse the tendency towards increasing inequality (Scheidel, 2018). To this rather disconcerting list, we might add (rather less disconcertingly) unionization of the workforce.

That market forces lead to increasing inequality is ironic considering that the supposedly well-known property of a market economy – that markets maximize aggregate welfare – rests on the assumption of approximate equality of income (Samuelson, 1956). This is because it is assumed that rational consumers will pay for any good or service what it is worth to them. However, in practice, many people lack the means to compete. Thus goods are purchased, not by those who value them the most, but those with the greatest means to pay. Indeed, Samuelson argued the free market will deliver goods inefficiently unless purchasing power (income and wealth) is approximately equalized across society, taking into account each person's basic needs. For example, elderly or ill people may require more resources as they have greater medical needs (and generally less income). Only after the equalizing of market power (for example, through generous pensions) can we rely on the market to produce an efficient result. It follows that the equality which the market requires in order to work smoothly is a prior condition, not a result, of free-market economics. However, even if all economic actors were to approach the market with an equal distribution of wealth and income, it is still not clear that market forces will guarantee optimal allocation of goods and services. This is because many markets are associated with externalities – that is, the benefits or costs of the purchase of goods and services will impact on the wellbeing of others (Bator, 1958).

Externalities and public goods

Negative externalities arise where market transactions cause costs to those not engaged in the transaction. A common example of a negative externality is the choice of private over public transport. Each person's decision to drive a car will impact on the level of costs paid by others in terms of time delays arising from increased congestion, increased likelihood of accidents and pollution. There also exist positive externalities, where (at least some of) the benefits arising from an action accrue to those not involved in the decision. Examples include education, job creation and technology spillover from research and development activity. Bator (1958, p 364) uses the example of apple blossom to discuss positive externalities (apple blossom being good both for the gardener and the beekeeper) and describes economic models which do not consider the impact of externalities as a 'dream world'.

It is well known that market forces will lead to an over-supply of goods and services which are associated with negative externalities and an under-supply of those goods and services associated with positive externalities. That is to say, left to itself, the market will produce, among other inefficiencies, an excess of pollution and private transportation and a deficit of education and jobs (and, one would speculate, insufficient apple blossom and bees).

Consider the positive externalities associated with employment. In a nation which provides some level of social security and employs some form of income tax, one person's income provides additional resources for the security of all. It follows the market will provide fewer than the optimal number of jobs, and at a lower than optimal rate of pay. One way around this would, of course, be to abandon taxation and social security – though this might not be politically acceptable in a democracy. Where citizens demand social security in return for their votes, an efficient outcome will only follow if the public sector intervenes in the labour market.

Another positive externality which arises from employment is the sense of community, self-worth and the health benefits which accrue to the employed (or at least, those securely employed in jobs which pay them enough to live), compared to the unemployed or those in precarious employment. It is in an attempt to capture these non-market benefits for their locale that national and local government may offer concessions to global firms to entice them to set up (or maintain existing) business. This is exacerbated by the global shortage of good employment. At this time of writing, less than half of the global workforce have access to 'good' jobs, according to some estimates (Clifton, 2019).

Externalities are not, to Bator (1958, p 352), the 'villain of the piece'. He reserves this epithet for public goods. Public goods are those where exclusion from use is not possible and the consumption by one does not diminish the amount of goods available to another. Thus the benefits of production go to all, whether they have contributed to the costs of production or not. An obvious example is the BBC – those who do not pay the licence are not physically excluded from watching (although they may be fined if caught). Other examples are street lighting, national and civil defence and the environment.

Public goods are not, of course, 'villains' as such – indeed, they are very much required in a well-functioning society – it is just that they will not be produced by the free market. Samuelson (1954, p 388) argues that where goods are public 'it is in the selfish interest of each person to give *false* signals' to the market (emphasis in original), so as to benefit from the good without contributing to the cost of production. This is known as the 'free rider' problem. Thus, acting purely in self-interest will lead to no contributions towards the cost of public goods, and therefore no production of a public good from which all would benefit.

In specific markets, government intervention may lead to an optimal allocation of public goods (for example, the BBC licence fee).[2] However, many public goods are non-market and therefore, even with government intervention, market transactions will lead to a sub-optimal allocation. Consider, for example, courtesy on the roads: risk-taking and discourteous drivers benefit from the consideration of those who have voluntarily chosen to limit their speed to safe levels, imposing on themselves the costs of longer journeys. In general, the broader concept of law and order benefits both those who respect it and those who do not. As a public good, law and order cannot and will not result from self-interested market transactions. In specific instances, of course, governments may intervene to create a disincentive for the most costly crimes (Becker, 1968). The point remains, with the free market comes the free-rider problem – if everyone acts solely in their own interest, very soon most public goods would cease to exist.

The need for social responsibility: private profits and public costs

In the context of our discussion of responsible innovation (RI), perhaps the most obvious public good is the global ecosystem itself. Those who are likely to suffer most from ecological change are not necessarily those who have contributed most to carbon dioxide in the Earth's atmosphere. This is partly a result of lifestyle differences, but also of how responsibility is allocated in mainstream economic theories, as discussed earlier. In leading free-market economies – such as the US, Japan, EU and UK – businesses generally pursue a two-pronged corporate strategy. Companies could, so far as is legally possible, maximize revenue by capturing the maximum return relative to what they produced – a direct result of their innovation investments. Alternatively, they could try to reduce operational risks and costs to the minimal levels legally acceptable and/or socially tolerable to their overall corporate strategy. Either strategy, or a combination of the two, seeks to grow and leverage an implicit social licence to operate (a form of social capital) and seek productive economic gains, thus maximizing profit.

The widespread adoption of such corporate strategies fosters a competitive industry where businesses individually seek to internalize (that is, retain) all the gains to their investments while attempting to keep at bay or externalize as much of the costs and negative consequences of their innovative actions as is legally possible, resulting in externalised costs to society. Some examples include polluting the environment, increasing traffic congestion, or maintaining product portfolios or manufacturing processes that are unsustainable in the longer term (thus passing costs onto future generations). Such a strategy is said to inherently privatize profit while socializing risk. Externalities (as discussed earlier) arise because of a significant failing of the market system; the market is often not able to effectively price-in the full value of certain economic activities. As a result, costs associated with specific commercial transactions are not usually fully internalized by the parties involved. Since corporate behaviour is optimized to capture as many positive benefits created as possible and avoid any associated adverse outcomes, it implies that 'transactional undesirables' become the responsibility of a third party or society in general, even though such third parties did not want to bear such risk exposures.

Innovation is at the heart of this behaviour. Companies use innovation to drive profit in ways that can capture the most customer patronage while minimizing operational costs and exposure to operational risk. The 2008 financial crisis is a case in point. As Stiglitz (2009) points out, the structure of global financial markets fuelled and incentivized companies in the financial industry to innovate and trade risky financial assets, without effectively pricing the associated risks into the returns on those assets for the investors and parties involved. If the pricing mechanism had adequately priced-in the full extent of the risk for over-securitized mortgage-backed securities, there would have been less demand for – and hence reduced transactions of – these financial instruments. The crisis might have been mitigated or even averted altogether. Billions in taxpayers' money might not have been spent to bail out 'too big to fail' financial businesses, thus avoiding austerity (or at least not providing the excuse for austerity). Taxpayers' money would, therefore, have been available to deal with pressing social issues, rather than withdrawn in a manner which precipitated further crises, such as an increase in homelessness. In short, it seems reasonable to say that the costs of those financial risks have been borne by society at large, while investors and others in global financial markets have continued to appropriate the benefits since.

A further illustration of these problems is sometimes called the 'tyranny of small decisions' (Kahn, 1966). Musing on the closure of the passenger railway services in Ithaca, NY, Kahn noted that, although the railway was not making money, its closure was an instance of market failure. To the residents of Ithaca, the possibility of using the railway was a public good in and of itself whether or not they used it sufficiently to make it profitable in terms of fares received. That is, they might have been prepared to pay to keep the railway running just in case they needed it, but the market mechanism only allowed payments for journeys taken. If Kahn had attempted a collection from local residents who would have benefited from maintaining the potential of using the railways, he would have found himself asking for donations towards a public good. Even those who value the presence of the railway would have no incentive to contribute their share – they could simply free-ride. Thus, the sum total of a large number of small, individually rational, decisions cumulates in an outcome which is both unforeseen and undesired. Even had the overall result been foreseen, there is no market solution.

A similar conundrum arises in the so-called tragedy of the commons (Hardin, 1968). This describes a situation where a freely available public good is degraded through overuse, the most obvious theoretic example being overgrazing privately owned animals on common land. While an individual might restrain their own use of the commons, restricting themselves to sustainability, the benefit of their restraint will largely accrue to all other commoners, and only in a small degree to themselves. Thus each will exercise less than the optimal amount of restraint (or none, resulting either in competition for an increasingly scarce resource, or the likelihood it becomes unable to sustain any grazing at all). The marketized approach to this problem is either to nationalize (and possibly ration) or (more likely) to privatize (that is, enclose) the commons. According to mainstream economic theory, this is because a single owner will have more incentive to preserve the resource for the future. Privatization is also favoured because it allows one entity to charge others for what was formerly free, thus creating a new market which can now contribute to (that is, be measured by) GDP, while the economic value of grazing rights on public land does not.

There is, however, an alternative non-market corrective to this 'tragedy', which is collective action reinforced by social norms (Ostrom, 1990). Through socially motivated restraint, public goods can be more effectively managed than through formal regulation or the dispossession of commoners from their rights. Although less about innovation (apart from the innovation required to create the social motivation), this reflects important aspects of responsible stagnation (RS), where 'living gently' and 'restraint' are part of creating not only new social norms, but the new incentives required to help people think cooperatively instead of competitively in maintaining public goods. We will discuss this and other kinds of 'social innovation' further in Chapter 5. However, it is worth taking a detour now to explore why this kind of cooperation is so difficult to motivate in the context of the market.

The Prisoners' Dilemma

One might think that people should be able to come together to solve their problems with markets (certainly this is the rationale underlying the idea of RI being aimed at the Grand Challenges of our time). However, game theory helps to explain why this is not always the case – at least if we stick to the economics of self-interest. The 'Prisoners' Dilemma' (Tucker and Straffin, 1983) is a form of economic thought experiment, in which the maximum social payoff is achieved if all cooperate. It supposes that two people are charged with jointly breaking the law, but held separately by the police and each offered the choice to confess or not. If they both confess, they both pay a fine of one unit. If one confesses (and implicates their 'partner in crime'), they will receive a reward of one unit, while the other pays a fine of two units. If neither confesses, then neither pays a fine. This trade-off is summarized in Table 3.1 where, in the brackets, the cost and benefit of Person I is on the left and that of Person II is on the right.

It is clear from the context of the game that the total cost to the partners is minimized if each upholds the code of 'honour among thieves' and refuses to confess. However, in the absence of knowledge of what the other plans to do, each individual is actually better off to default on their code of honour and turn the other in. Thus, each undermines the other's chance of escaping punishment. Even though, overall, both are better off cooperating, individually each is better off to pursue their own self-interest, and thus the most socially costly outcome is the one most likely to be adopted.

Table 3.1: The Prisoners' Dilemma

		Person II	
		Confess	Don't confess
Person I	Confess	(-1,-1)	(1,-2)
	Don't confess	(-2,1)	(0,0)

Source: Authors' own work, based on Tucker and Straffin, 1983

The Prisoners' Dilemma does not only describe the actions of crime suspects, of course. Rather, it describes all situations where cooperation is required to achieve a joint goal, but where (in the absence of an appropriate means to enforce cooperation) each individual is better off not to cooperate, irrespective of what the other chooses to do. While this is true of prisoners, it is also true of many social decisions. Consider the provision of public goods, such as a sustainable ecosystem. While each individual is better off if ecological change does not occur, they are even better off if all others restrain their consumption choices while they themselves indulge in whatever they wish. We see, then, that simple self-interest is not sufficient to take us to a welfare maximizing outcome where one person's decisions will impact on the wellbeing of others. This is the essential problem which arises from competitive markets. An obvious example, current at time of writing, is the decision an individual makes about whether or not to engage in social distancing during a global pandemic.

For another example, consider the case of Australian domestic flights between the 1940s and the 1990s, when the government enforced a Two Airlines policy. Now imagine the government introduces a new $50 per sector tax for all domestic flights. The companies must decide whether to pass this on to passengers and raise prices, or absorb the tax and keep their fares as they were. If both airlines pass the tax on, their profits and customer share will remain unchanged. If neither pass the tax on, they will retain the same share of customers they had before the tax, but will have reduced profits. If only one passes it on but the other absorbs it, the one that passes the tax on will have higher-priced flights compared to the one that does not, and will lose customers to the one absorbing the tax, and hence lose some profit, while the one absorbing the tax will gain market share, and (in this case) increase its profit. This trade-off is summarized in Table 3.2, with the changes in profit for Airline I on the left and that of Airline II on the right.

As with the classic Prisoners' Dilemma, overall the airlines would be better off if both passed on the tax (where they would have no loss of profit or market share). But individually, without knowing what the other is likely to do, each is actually better

Table 3.2: The Airlines' Dilemma

		Airline II	
		Pass tax	Absorb tax
Airline I	Pass tax	(0,0)	(-2M,+1M)
	Absorb tax	(+1M,-2M)	(-1M,-1M)

Source: Authors' own work

off absorbing the tax. This may seem the opposite of what we expect (and frankly, what airlines generally do!) but in theory, it is the safer option. The model suggests they should both settle on absorbing the tax, and thus the most costly outcome is again adopted (although better from the customer's point of view). It is possible to also think of this as the Innovation Dilemma, a particular problem for small businesses with fragile market shares. If one business innovates and the others do not, there is a possibility of growth through expanding the market share. However, if each business engages in costly innovation, and all others do too, there may be no new customers to gain, especially in a niche market. Thus, businesses are not always incentivized to innovate, and when they do, they may run the risk of pricing themselves out of competition unless they are able to absorb the costs. We will return to this idea in Chapter 7.

Before we leave the Prisoners' Dilemma, it is worth considering how airlines may find their way out of the dilemma; how they may, in short, pass on the tax. This is possible because in practice, many such dilemmas are not one-off, they are actually repeating games in which, if one participant pursues a strategy of self-interest and the other does not, the potential for retaliation exists in the next round.

This strategy, to play 'nice' – that is, to pursue a cooperative policy – in the first round and continue to play nice only as long as the other participant also played nice in the previous round, but to default if the other participant defaulted, is known as 'tit for tat'. It has been shown to be optimal in an ongoing (that is, infinitely repeating) Prisoners' Dilemma game. To apply such a strategy requires, however, not only that the game be ongoing, but also that each player knows when the other has dealt them 'tat'. It also requires each to have the ability to deliver sufficient 'tat' in the next round if retaliation is required (thus assuming an endlessly escalating series of retaliations).

One route out of this ongoing tit-for-tat Prisoners' Dilemma, therefore, is an agreement by both parties (or regulation of both parties) to play 'nice', along with transparency in outcomes and an appropriate punishment strategy. In short, we must be able to assess responsibility and there must be some means of holding the irresponsible to account. It is not enough to rely on goodwill, yet some goodwill is essential if we are not to remain stuck in a tit-for-tat spiral that ultimately benefits no one.

Is economic growth really growth?

All this is not to say we ought to do away with markets, of course. We ought, however, to limit their use to the things at which they are best and adopt non-market solutions where appropriate. However, even the question of when market-based solutions are appropriate is by no means clear. It depends on our overall policy objective. It is to this issue we now turn. We will argue that, as a policy objective, the pursuit of economic growth, as indicated by increases in headline GDP, is flawed (Fioramonti, 2017). In particular, we attempt to draw a distinction between wealth creation and wealth appropriation. With the former, of course, we have no issue. It is the latter that becomes problematic.

'Economic growth' is often defined as increases in a nation's (or planetary) Gross Domestic Product (GDP), despite the fact that this does not necessarily measure all of the economic activity which occurs in any given locale (much of which takes place outside the market). It is also neither the only, or even the best, measure of whether a nation's economy is truly healthy or not (for example, GDP may grow due to siphoning wealth from the poor to the rich, or from the commons to the individual). GDP loosely corresponds to the monetary value of goods and services produced (or purchased) over a period of time (for example, over a year). 'Real GDP' denotes this figure adjusted for the effects of price inflation.

Consideration of GDP indicates straight away that it is a less than ideal measure of a nation's wellbeing as it does not include non-market goods and services, such as parents looking after their own children, growing and/or cooking one's own food, or non-monetary exchanges such as giving things away instead of selling them second-hand. In addition, it does not provide a measure of human aspirations at anything but the lowest needs. Once physiological and security needs are met, increased marketized consumption may do little to facilitate the meeting of higher needs such as social belonging, self-esteem, self-actualization and, ultimately, transcendence (altruism and/or spirituality).

This is not to say, of course, that increases in the income of the economically vulnerable might not improve their wellbeing. Indeed, they are likely to benefit most if their income increases. However, as discussed in Chapter 1, there is a diminishing marginal benefit to a one unit growth in income. Notwithstanding that those with greater financial resources demonstrate greater wellbeing overall than those with less, beyond a certain point, increasing national income does not appear to be related to an increase in national wellbeing. An obvious example is the US, where GDP was continually increasing from 2008 to 2019, yet real median wages did not increase, so that poverty, inequality and social unrest had become serious problems, even before the onset of the COVID-19 pandemic.

This is because, in a free market, each individual is motivated to pursue growth in their own income, even though there may be no benefit to that growth at a national level. This would not matter if GDP growth merely related to the sum of value added (that is, the monetary value of output less any inputs) but it does not. In practice, many of the inputs into GDP are wrongly assumed to be free, when in fact they are not. Thus, there might be no national benefit arising from GDP growth, but instead such (so-called) growth arises from incurring significant national costs.

Consider production and consumption in a 'closed' ecosystem, such as the Earth. This ecosystem can import an amount of energy (for example sunlight) every year at zero-cost, but other than that, neither imports nor exports anything. Output is comprised of two parts: a portfolio of goods and services required by people for their wellbeing; and an increase in knowledge (or technical ability) which will allow more efficient production (that is, reduced per unit cost) of goods and services in the future.

The value of this ecosystem can be calculated as the net discounted present value of current and future wellbeing which can be obtained from it. Hence, anything which reduces the prospects of the maintenance of wellbeing in the future reduces the value of the Earth. However, while GDP measures the cost of transforming power or raw materials and the cost of producing knowledge and labour, it does not take into account the reduction in stocks of raw materials which remain. For example, part of the cost of burning irreplaceable (under current technology) fossil fuel today is that we cannot then burn the same units of fuel tomorrow; part of the cost of fishing unsustainably today is that there will be fewer fish tomorrow. Such costs are not accounted for anywhere in GDP calculations. GDP, in short, does not properly account for the cost of primary inputs. The fact that these costs will certainly impact our descendants is ignored; a severe lack of responsibility which RI is, in part, hoping to address through a 'collective commitment of care for the future' in the shaping of innovation today (Owen et al, 2013b, p 36).

Neither does GDP adequately reflect the reduction in future wellbeing which results from nations and individuals taking on debt today. This is particularly pertinent as, in many Western nations, debt had been increasing at a faster rate than GDP, even before the 2020 global pandemic. Recall that GDP may be defined as the sum value of goods and services circulating (or, if you prefer, consumption and investment) in the economy. If an increase in national expenditure (supposedly indicating growth) must be financed by an even greater increase in national debt, it is by no means clear that this should be interpreted as a sign of improving prospects. Yet, exploitation of a new oilfield, clear-felling a forest to graze beef, or debt-fuelled consumption are all regarded as economic activities to be stimulated if they add to current GDP, irrespective of the cost a future generation might bear as a result of these developments.

Clearly then, a lot of what is considered 'wealth creation' under current national accounting mechanisms is in fact wealth *destruction* when viewed from the point of view of the long-term wellbeing of the inhabitants of the planet. In particular, a great deal of real stagnation (even decrease) in prosperity and future economic prospects might be hidden from view by the national accounting abstraction that increases in GDP represent.

Beyond Gross Domestic Product

Since GDP confuses wealth destruction with wealth creation, it is clearly an inadequate measure of progress. We might consider, as an alternative, a measure such as the Ecological Footprint (Mancini et al, 2016; Wiedmann and Minx, 2007), which takes into account the future cost of current activities. By this measure, the Earth has been in deficit (that is, compromising its future wellbeing) since the 1970s, and by 2019 we were consuming the assets of the world at a rate in excess of 60 per cent above the long-term carrying capacity of the planet.

Other alternatives to GDP exist, for example, the Genuine Progress Index and Index of Sustainable Economic Welfare (Lawn, 2003). These weight GDP by income distribution (less equality reduces the index), unpaid work (for example volunteering, household work and care work all add to the index) and subtract the environmental and social costs of production. According to Jackson and McBride (2005), taking into account such factors ignored by GDP calculations indicates the UK has had a stagnant economy since the mid 1970s, as have many other developed economies, including the US. This stagnation in real beneficial growth – though not GDP – is not limited to the developed world, but is rather a global phenomenon (Kubiszewski et al, 2013).

Given the current global context, the reader may be concerned that, in proposing ideas which consider 'stagnation' as responsible, we are proposing policies that will mean little, if any, improvement in wellbeing. We argue it is already clear that on a global level wellbeing is already stagnant, and has been for four decades. We have, in fact, been in a state of *irresponsible* stagnation, exacerbated by the adoption of socio-political policies primarily concerned with increasing GDP irrespective of the impact of this on social cohesion and long-term prosperity. Our current choice appears to be not between responsible and irresponsible *innovation*, but between irresponsible stagnation and supporting innovation in its broadest sense, combined with frameworks aimed at taking more responsibility for where we go from here, rather than leaving it to the market to decide. This allows us to seek the best social impact regardless of contribution to GDP, in order to address the fundamental inability of the market to allocate the benefits of growth to all. Creating policies which emphasize increasing wellbeing and sustainability might very well increase GDP, and to this we do not object, but this cannot be their primary objective.

This is why we have chosen to embrace the term 'RS' and explore what it might truly mean. It is clear that political leaders can no longer rely on net growth to deliver social progress; rather, it appears reasonable to suppose instead that global real net income may be (at best) stable. According to Adam Smith (1806, p 128), in such a situation, that is when an economy reaches its limits of growth, 'the competition for employment would necessarily be so great as to reduce the wages of labour to what was barely sufficient to keep up the number of labourers'. In other words, in this kind of market equilibrium, the economy is marked both by low wages and low profits as producers suffer from high charges for finance, or 'enormous usury', as Smith (1806, p 127) terms it. We might rather say 'rents extracted by financialisation', but otherwise the description fits our current economic climate very well.

There is one aspect Smith overlooked, however, which is the decline in the number of labourers needed. We know there is a global lack of good jobs, or as an economist would say, a global lack of demand for labour. As economies continue to increase productivity through technological innovation, this situation is likely to worsen (Keynes, 1963). In response to this shortfall in demand, market forces have reduced wages below the level at which the stock of labour (that is, the working-age population) is stable in many developed nations. If this were not the case, governments would have little need of minimum or living-wage regulations, or in-work benefits for those who are employed full-time, but earn below a living wage. The social consequences of a sizeable proportion of the public not being able to afford to subsist, no matter how hard they work (if they can find work at all), are not conducive to sustainable nations.

However, there are other pathways we could follow, even within an economy which still depends mainly on market activity. As Mill notes, even without growth, in a stable economy where population is also stable and *inequality is constrained* we might expect to see

> a well-paid and affluent body of labourers; no enormous fortunes, except what were earned and accumulated during a single lifetime; but a much larger body of persons than at present, not only exempt from the coarser toils, but with sufficient leisure, both physical and mental, from mechanical details, to cultivate freely the graces of life. (Mill, 1909, p 750)

This sounds much more appealing (except, perhaps to some, Mill's requirement of no enormous fortunes!) A similar conclusion was reached by the great British economist of the 20th century, John Maynard Keynes (1963), who forecast, in 1930, a future in which a 15-hour working week would be sufficient to produce all that civilization requires. However, this would require hourly wages, leisure and standards of living to increase for all (rather than decline, as they have for many), and a concerted effort to both improve productivity (in the sense of conserving vital resources) and decrease unnecessary consumption (that is, things whose absence would not significantly impact on our wellbeing). This is part of what we mean by 'RS'.

Unfortunately, according to Keynes (echoing Smith), the prerequisites for such a future involve the establishment of some very different social norms to those we currently display. These include a 'return to some of the most sure and certain principles of ... traditional virtue – that avarice is a vice, that the exaction of usury is a misdemeanour, and the love of money is detestable' (Keynes, 1963, p 211). Clearly such a progressive set of norms is unlikely to be delivered by a marketplace which emphasizes the continual pursuit of individual self-interest.

In this chapter we have argued that the free market will, over time, erode the equality on which its supposed efficiency rests. However, even if there were perfect equality of resources, there would still be a need to regulate markets – whether formally through democratically accountable government or socially through the establishing of appropriate norms – as there are many problems which markets are simply not able to solve. This analysis should not be taken as implying that market-based capitalism has not created growth – merely that, in the long run, the less regulated the market, the fewer there will be who benefit from this growth.

Increasing inequality has social and economic implications. As Benjamin Friedman (2006) points out, when a society is achieving material progress for the broad cross-section of its people, that is when it is also most able, and most likely, to make progress in moral dimensions such as racial tolerance. As broadly based growth (that is, growth which benefits most, if not all, citizens) delivers positive externalities (such as tolerance), he argues that an optimal rate of economic growth cannot be delivered solely by the market. This is why our concept of innovation must be broader than that which takes place within the market, and must be directed at ways to *reduce* (or stagnate) throughput where necessary.

We have argued that both the tools by which we might pursue economic growth, the so-called free market, and indeed the definition of growth itself, are inadequate in our current global situation. Governments whose policies are informed by the prevailing globalized free-market ideology are less likely to interfere in the workings of the market, and thus inequality is increasing in the (so-called) developed world, resulting in rising intolerance in our societies and reversing decades of social progress. What new policies may arise from the COVID-19 crisis cannot, as of this writing, yet be seen. However, insofar as income growth accrues to those least in need of more, or represents only corporate spending, it is essentially inefficient at best and undermining of wellbeing at worst.

There is little evidence of sustainable growth in any event. Although it is possible to increase GDP metrics in the short- to medium-term by, for example, burning yet more fossil fuels, engaging in unsustainable economic activities, and/or borrowing yet more from the future, globally we have experienced no net economic progress since the late 1970s. By discounting future wellbeing, and failing to take into account the negative externalities of GDP activity, political and business leaders have inadvertently compromised the sustainability of our economic, ecological and social structures.

The global socio-economic system has reached (at best) a situation of economic stagnation, whether we acknowledge it or not. Reflecting on the causes of the 2008 Global Financial Crisis, Lanchester (2010, p 232) similarly concludes, 'In a world running out of resources, the most important ethical, political, and ecological idea can be summed up in the simple word "enough"'.

As we go forward from the entwined health and economic crises of 2020, political leaders and the populations they represent effectively face a choice of facilitating increased leisure (a good measure of prosperity) or facing increased social unrest. Down which route nations travel will depend on the approach taken towards sharing the benefits of the global economy. To truly enable RI, governments will need to ensure that market forces are adequately constrained so as to benefit society, both in the present and in the future. Such a government cannot consider the free market as an appropriate means of achieving social progress, nor GDP as its appropriate measure. It is for this reason that we propose an a-growth approach to innovation, and to take seriously the possibilities of RS.

PART III

Responsible Stagnation and the Real World

Having set the landscape and its challenges, it's time to journey across this landscape and see what ways there are to move forward.

We begin this journey with an exploration of the notion of responsibility, and what the underlying values of responsible stagnation (RS) might be. We start by considering the challenge of uncertainty in innovation, and the centrality of process in decision-making. Specifically, we note the importance of allowing sufficient time and of acting with care in our decision-making process. We show how, at its core, RS offers a new lens for viewing the relationship between society and science, research, technology and innovation.

We then continue by taking a closer look at how RS interacts with three real-world contexts: social innovation, the Global South and corporations. First, we will look at a range of social innovations which are centred primarily on new ways of creating social value or responding to social needs often not met by standard market-based activities, reflecting a tacit commitment to care and connection as important motivating values.

Next, we turn our attention to the Global South as a way to think more deeply through the political implications of innovation on a wider scale. Starting with an appreciation that technology does not consist of neutral 'mere' tools, but can be used as an instrument of persuasion and domination, we discuss how innovation policies and our imagining of what counts as innovation can be (and has been) used as a form of colonial domination. The aspirations of RS, and especially a 'commitment to care', are used to reconsider the relationship between innovation and geo-political structures, recognizing that the Global South represents a great reservoir of localized, alternative ways of framing innovation.

Finally, we turn to the possibilities and challenges for RS in guiding corporate behaviour. While innovation policy is generally enacted through universities, research institutes and other state-funded initiatives, much of the research and development (R&D) that drives innovation actually takes place in the private sector. Issues here include the purpose of corporate social responsibility programmes, and demands arising due to shareholder-stakeholder dichotomies and public accountability measures. We will also explore Benefit Corporations (B Corps) as existing alternative corporate structures which already enable a form of RS in business, and how such structures can support a much more expansive idea of responsibility, even within the for-profit corporate sector.

4

Putting Responsibility Centre Stage: The Underlying Values of Responsible Stagnation

Fabien Medvecky

As we have seen in Part I, innovation is often lauded as the saviour we desperately need, as if it is some kind of knight in shining armour astride his noble steed, Market Economy, capable of redressing all the injustices of world. Sometimes, it is acknowledged, the knight doesn't deliver quite as we hoped and some readjustments are needed – enter the faithful squire, Responsibility. But when the knight is more like Don Quixote, tilting at non-existent giants, and the market is more akin to his horse Rocinante (who was too far past its use-by date to fulfil its tasks), to keep replacing the fallen hero in his saddle isn't enough.

As we have seen in Chapter 3, the market economy is, in fact, not shaped to deliver what we expect from a supposedly prosperous society (namely real social progress and benefits, such as genuine wage growth, better environmental outcomes and so on). So what happens if we rid our hero of the steed and we meet our knight on foot, with no expectation of any specific outcome for Gross Domestic Product (GDP)? Taking this agnosticism to GDP as our starting point – what van den Bergh (2011) calls the 'a-growth' paradigm – we ask what happens now when our knight Innovation meets his squire Responsibility? What becomes possible once we stop trying to ride the market and instead innovate independent of market-directed aspirations? In Chapter 2, we saw how Responsible Research and Innovation (RRI) emerged from responses to the inadequacy of modern structures to deal responsibly with science and technology (S&T)-induced risks and uncertainties, situations often characterized by disputed underlying values, social and/or epistemic resistance and conflicts, and urgent political decisions. Although RRI/RI opens science, technology and innovation (STI) to broader public debate and seeks to integrate various kinds of expertise (technical, sociological, lay) into decision-making about specific technologies, RI alone cannot sufficiently address societal, ethical and ecological concerns about broader STI processes, nor how these are shaped by, and respond to, externalities in the global political economy. So long as RI is embedded in the GDP growth paradigm, it risks only ever rearranging Don Quixote in his saddle rather than calling forth a better knight (whatever that might be). So let us instead put responsibility centre stage and see what happens if we rethink RI. Let's leave the horse aside and re-imagine our knight.

Insofar as RI is a policy innovation, anticipating and being reflexive about the potential risks and benefits of RI itself is essential if it is to achieve its loftier goals. RI discourse is partially shaped by the assumption that publicly funded basic research will be taken up by industry–university partnerships and developed into goods and services to be sold through spin-outs. One possible detrimental impact is the increasing burden placed upon scientists as RI becomes a requirement for research funding at both UK and EU levels, particularly when coupled with demands to produce research which can be commercialized (Holloway, 2015). Emergent technologies such as nano- or biotechnology promise to feed, warm and heal, as well as enrich, through the creation of GDP wealth and high-tech, well-paid jobs. However, there is a danger that by claiming to have already anticipated and reflected on negative impact 'upstream' while promissory research is still being done, RI will instead redouble efforts to get these technologies to the market as quickly as possible, before effective resistance movements can be formed (Singh,

2008). Some areas of research have already generated so much public unease, particularly about the quality and effectiveness of regulation, that attempts to commercialize it have been forcibly (and in some opinions, irresponsibly) stagnated by widespread resistance. In particular, worry over the 'failed' attempt to commercialize GM in Europe still lurks behind much of the discussion of RI, including from a significant proportion of policy makers (see EC, 2013, p 14).

However, history also shows us that in certain instances, policy makers and scientists *have* chosen forms of what might be called stagnation – a slowdown or cessation of activity – as the most responsible course of action in the face of uncertainty and public unease about their research. The voluntary moratorium on recombinant DNA research in the early 1970s (Berg, 2008), the near world-wide ban on human reproductive cloning (UN, 2005), and the cessation of gain-of-function research on deadly viruses (US, 2014) all suggest that science does sometimes accept that some research trajectories should remain stagnant, at least for a time. The Precautionary Principle advocates a similar approach of slowing down in the face of uncertainty, and giving a larger weight to potential negative impact than to potential positive returns.

In his masterwork, *The Great Transformation*, Karl Polanyi suggested that, 'It should need no elaboration that a process of undirected change, the pace of which is deemed too fast, should be slowed down, if possible, so as to safeguard the welfare of the community' (Polyani, 2001, pp 32–3).

These ideas, we would suggest, also form an important underpinning of our idea of responsible stagnation (RS). Polanyi's work argues that economics is a set of social relationships. Where these relationships have become 'disembedded' and monetary interests outweigh social interests, capitalism may provide wealth for a few, but unevenly so, and often at an enormous cost for the rest. This, we suggest, is exactly where our present ideas about innovation and growth have taken us.

As discussed in Chapter 1, the Fourth Quadrant of the innovation matrix comprises two overriding questions: how do we innovate responsibly in economies which may be in a permanent state of slow growth, and if innovation for stagnation can contribute to the maintenance of prosperity, how do we do this responsibly? It is not enough simply for innovation to be restrained by responsibility; we want to advocate for responsibility as the *driver* of innovation. While RI says 'innovate, but do so responsibly', RS says 'innovate *because* of our responsibilities'.

In short, as the emphasis changes, the consideration of responsibilities become an enabler, an inspiration and a motivator, not a constraint. In this, we see RS working alongside, not in opposition to, RI frameworks, strengthening the potential to address the conflicting messages from a political establishment simultaneously demanding both austerity and growth. The incompatibility of these objectives suggests that as social actors, politicians, academics and economists are as conflicted as the average person about how to achieve a sustainable future (Bryan et al, 2012) precisely because our present discourses make it so difficult to think beyond growth.

We suggest first that in order to achieve a 'proper embedding' of innovation in society (von Schomberg, 2013, p 39), RS in the form of slowing down, stopping or changing course needs to be incorporated into the discussion of RI as a reasonable response, so that social and ecological costs and benefits have equal, if not more, importance than projected possible economic returns. RI suggests itself partly as a decision-making endeavour, allowing a debate of impacts, benefits and motivations for technological development to occur far upstream, before innovation pathways are set. This would imply that its main activities take place at a point where multiple pathways are still possible. In this context, considering stagnation as a genuine option could allow for a wider debate, a broader set of policy options about the role of innovation in our economic system and the real-world consequences of continuing to seek productivity growth. It would also allow for deeper consideration of our underlying economic assumptions, models and ways of producing knowledge, opening these up for interrogation (as has been the case with the natural sciences).

Thinking more deeply about the interaction of economic assumptions and their relationship to innovation invites a reflective turn on RI itself. We have so far argued that the present socio-technical political economy relies upon the parallel assumptions that innovation and growth are always good, therefore more and faster innovation and growth must be better. Within this single-minded responsibility to innovate to increase GDP, RI can do little to question whether growth in a given context is truly desirable, or even necessary for a flourishing society, let alone whether a risky innovation pathway can achieve its projected goals. Not only is it not clear *when* the costs of the 'disruption' outweigh the benefits of the 'creation', the issue is not even considered. STI policy continues to seek 'disruptive innovation' yet crucial questions about the result of such disruption cannot be asked.

It is unlikely RI will achieve its objective of socially beneficial innovation to solve complex problems if RI itself cannot question its own normative conditions and whether it might need to change its own trajectory, or consider whether certain pathways and technologies are too environmentally or socially costly to pursue. By challenging the assumption that innovation and growth are always good, the Fourth Quadrant provides a space in which we can ask the kinds of questions about RS we dared not, but perhaps should have been, asking all along.

The concept of 'responsibility' in responsible stagnation

RS, like any framework, brings with it its own set of concepts and values. It's time we dive into these by asking two questions that look at specific aspects of RS. To begin with, while RS might challenge the traditional rhetoric around the inherent value of innovation, RS also maintains a commitment to responsibility in STI endeavours. So the primary question is: 'what does the concept of "responsibility" mean or look like in RS?'

Secondly, by suggesting that innovation is not always or necessarily an unquestionable good, RS makes it explicit that all STI endeavours and policies have underlying value assumptions, and that any such assumptions ought to be regularly revisited. But RS itself also has underlying value assumptions; most evident are the values of precaution, democratic accountability and a commitment to environmental values and equitable social conditions. And as much as it is important to be clear and explicit about the values underlying STI endeavours and policy, it is equally important to be clear about the values underlying RS, so the second question we ask is exactly this: 'what are the underlying values of RS and how are they envisaged?'

The classic framing of RI in the innovation landscape calls for us to be anticipatory, reflective, inclusively deliberative and responsive (Owen et al, 2013a). RS enlarges this to encompass action beyond being responsive to the specific instance in question or simply including more of the public. Instead (as discussed in Chapter 2), we also need to be able to reflect upon, and be responsive to, the larger political economy in which our innovating is taking place, and to be inclusive of a greater diversity of ideas, paradigms and norms, as well as people.

Responsible decision-making with regard to technology and innovation is particularly challenging for a number of reasons, the most prominent ones being the inherent high level of uncertainty over outcomes and the increased speed of innovation. Put simply, technology and innovation moves much faster than our capacity to assess and understand long-term outcomes and effects, or to mitigate them once apparent. When making decisions with such uncertain, unpredictable outcomes as those coming out of novel research and emerging technology, simply ensuring responsibility through regulation and oversight often falls short, and more encompassing processes for being responsible must be called upon. This is the basis of RI, which RS also supports.

Grinbaum and Groves (2013) specifically point to new approaches that they term 'quasi-parental responsibility' and 'collective political responsibility', which includes RI. Collective responsibility implies having a shared responsibility for an action or outcome stemming from the fact that the decision to pursue the original action was collective. As Owen and colleagues remind us, 'responsible innovation is ultimately about being responsible, taking responsibility, and innovating responsibly: but this is a collective endeavour' (Owen et al, 2013b, p 46). In principle, RI renders the decision to pursue a certain innovation 'collective' by ensuring that social actors are involved throughout the innovation process, a point which may go some way towards mitigating the concerns over the 'tragedy of the commons' discussed in Chapter 3 by assigning responsibility to everyone, rather than no one. But the challenge over uncertainty remains; the collective is not necessarily better at reliably knowing or predicting the outcome of scientific and technological innovation than innovators themselves. Indeed, whether the game is oversight, individual responsibility or collective responsibility, working out what the right approach to *assessing* if one is being responsible is a messy endeavour, let alone actually *being* responsible!

Let's start by considering possibilities for assessing whether an agent (either an individual or a collective) is 'being responsible' with regard to research and innovation. Van de Poel and Sand (2018) conclude that two types of responsibility are particularly important in relation to responsible innovation (RI), namely accountability and responsibility-as-virtue. Where evaluation is carefully applied, such an approach may be suitable to assigning responsibility, but this is particularly difficult with regard to innovation. Collingridge (1981) has identified this as a dilemma whereby research and innovation can be influenced in the early stages, but at this point the risks and benefits are difficult to foresee because there is not yet enough information. Simultaneously, once the technologies or innovations are advanced enough to allow meaningful consideration of their social, environmental and economic implications, they are already so deeply embedded in society that it's no longer possible to meaningfully change direction or use. Facebook and Cambridge Analytica serve as a prime example. In the early years after Facebook's foundation, it is likely that no one foresaw how the technology's business model of collecting data on its users' activities could be used to inappropriately interfere in electoral processes, as Cambridge Analytica did in both the US and the UK in 2016. Now, Facebook is such a ubiquitous technology, and the sale of its users' data so central to its business model, that it does not appear possible to curb this behaviour in any meaningful way.

The importance of time and timing with regard to RI is strangely lost in the current innovation landscape. From a moral decision-making standpoint, the implication of the Collingridge Dilemma is that any appeal to consequentialism (that is, using consequences as *the* measure of moral evaluation) is doomed to fail when it comes to making sense of responsibility in research and innovation. Given that the consequences of STI decisions cannot be used as the measure of responsible behaviour because it is usually either too early to foresee the consequences or too late to be meaningfully addressed, a more promising approach is to look at the decision-making process itself. If we cannot ensure a responsible *outcome*, we must instead try to ensure that the *process* used for making decisions is responsible, given the context in which the decision is made. This rationale sits at the core of RI, and remains important for RS. What matters is not just consequences, but the decision-making process itself – in other words, the end *doesn't* always justify the means, particularly when we cannot know what the end might look like once we're there. Responsibility, therefore, becomes about having a responsible process for making decisions about how we proceed.

With this in mind, RI (and its predecessors discussed in Chapter 2) has aspired to nudge the research and innovation community away from the insulation of the laboratory to be more public-facing. Ideally, researchers and innovators now have to ask themselves as well as the broader public about 'the wider social and political significance of what they intend to accomplish, and what [their] actions may accomplish despite [their] intentions' (Grinbaum and Groves, 2013, p 133).

While such paradigm shifts in responsibility for STI are laudable, these are still far from ideal processes for responsible decision-making. The current processes are aimed at furthering and bettering innovation first and foremost, not at driving responsibility as the core principle for our actions. As Blok and Lemmens (2015, p 20) point out, this can reduce responsibility to 'an add-on or extension to the concept of innovation; responsible innovation = regular innovation + stakeholder involvement with regard to ethical and societal aspects'. Such an add-on or extension comes with a tension between speeding up and slowing down. RI requires time and effort, which is against the prevailing policy discourse of seeking ways to remove barriers and reduce regulation in order to speed up the innovation process.

Responsibility + innovation or responsibility versus innovation?

The interpretation of 'responsibility' as embodied in the RI literature – interpreting responsibility as processes that improve or progress innovation – creates a tension around time and timeframes. It takes time to anticipate, to meaningfully include other stakeholders and other options, to reflect and decide what actions can or should be taken in response; it takes time to have response-*ability*. And it takes time to think carefully through issues, it takes mental grunt-work, and it's a process we do less often than we'd like to admit (Kahneman, 2011). On the other hand, innovation as it is usually defined in the business literature – bringing goods and services to market, individually motivated by the pursuit of profit, and politically underpinned by a GDP growth-creating agenda – occurs in an increasingly unstable competitive environment, underpinned by concepts such as efficiency (the paradoxical doing-more-with-less), flexibility (or disposability) and agility (fast reaction), all of which impart a sense of unconstrained urgency. Indeed, 'strategic agility', now a core value for many firms, is very much about enabling faster decision-making. This includes 'the internal capability to reconfigure capabilities and redeploy resources rapidly' (Doz and Kosonen, 2010). So here is the tension for RI: *responsibility* often requires that we slow down, take time, be careful and thoughtful in our decision-making, and this needs to be reflected in our process for the latter to be considered responsible. *Innovation*, by contrast, lives primarily in a world driven by competitive urgency and rapid flexibility: don't waste time! Act fast or your competitors will beat you! This makes RI less 'innovation + responsibility' and more 'innovation vs responsibility'. To break this tension, we need to think of innovation beyond the kind of market-driven techno-scientific innovation we usually have in mind when calling on RI. Thus RS!

The value of slowed reasoning

As we saw in Chapter 1, RS begins not only with an examination of economics and growth, but also by questioning how the term 'innovation' is understood and interpreted in RI. Through this interrogation, innovation is viewed more broadly than solely bringing goods to market. As previously noted, RS defines innovation as 'the process by which novelty is taken up and circulated in the public sphere (including the application of something existing to something entirely different), producing some kind of profound re-ordering of what-has-been' (de Saille & Medvecky, 2016, p 7). While this definition does not exclude innovations that arise in a competitive, market-driven environment, it also extends into the space outside of the market environment, allowing inclusion of numerous non-market innovations that aim at reducing throughput or filling social needs as well. This decoupling of RI and innovation from the growth agenda breaks the tension arising out of the market imperative usually linked to RI, and allows us both the time and space to enact 'responsibility'.

Because we cannot reiterate this often enough: responsibility in RS is not contrary to the notion of responsibility in RI, it is a complement to it. By inviting a broader rethink of innovation, RS provides a greater ability to respond; or, to use Blok's and Lemmens' (2015) wording, improves 'the response-*ability* of actors in the innovation process'. While most of us (usually) aim to act responsibly and morally, and we certainly largely believe that we do, we actually spend very little time reasoning about it *prior* to acting. We're much more likely to slow down and think about why we've done what we've done *after* we've acted, and usually with a focus on justifying our decisions rather than guiding them (Haidt, 2001). Therefore, while many of the concerns underpinning RI are reflected in RS's conceptualization of notion of responsibility, what RS stresses – apart from removing the market-driven objective from the core of innovation – is the imperative for stagnating the *doing* until some prior reasoning has been seriously had. RS, by putting responsibility centre stage, demands we make time for good decision-making. 'Anticipatory, reflective, inclusively deliberative, and responsive', yes, of course, but with *slowed reasoning*. Slow enough to allow the necessary time to reflect and consider the options available, their possible consequences and the values espoused by all involved, even if it means a delay in getting to the market. Slowed reasoning so there is time to change course or even stop entirely if this is indicated.

Importantly, we don't mean *always* slowing down the innovation process per se. In some cases, we might well want to speed up innovation for social, economic or environmental reasons. RS is about slowing down the reflective component of the decision-making process. The outcome of slower, more reflective decision-making might well lead to faster, more certain, concerted action *once the decisions have been made*. RS asks us to take more care with our decision-making, to make fast decisions when there is a need for them (such as in a pandemic), and to take the time we need when we have it (which we usually do). It asks us to consider what we cannot undo and what we may no longer be able to do once we've made our decisions.

The underlying values of responsible stagnation and governance with care

We opened this book with the premise that we should not assume *a-priori* the desirability of economic growth and should not pursue innovation for its own sake, since limitless economic growth of the kind defined as increasing GDP (that is to say, a perpetually increasing cost of monetized transactions) is both unsustainable and not necessarily just. Having established that allowing time to make careful decisions is central to RS, what are the underlying values we then ought to use to guide our decision-making?

In our introduction, we presented five ideas or principles that underpin RS. Firstly, RS is not the knight to replace our ailing Don Quixote. It is not the answer to tilting at windmills, but a space in which to travel, one that opens up possibilities and allows for more substantive kinds of questions to be asked, and unshackled answered to be suggested. It is a **pool of great ideas**, some old, some new – to continue our metaphor, more often bordered by existing inns than imaginary castles. RS, more than anything, describes a **particular configuration of change** in which **ethics matters** as a crucial axis of decision-making. In line with 'slowed reasoning', if RS advocates for any particular ethical approach to innovation it is one of **restraint**, both in the innovation process and in the implementation of innovation, with an eye to the interplay of policy, economic activities and the kind of society this technology might shape. Above all, to be responsible in a world with ecological limits, we need to seek innovation which enables **living gently** upon the Earth and with each other, rather than seeking new ways to maximize our benefits regardless of costs.

However, while living gently, thoughtfully and with restraint is a good way of making ethics matter, we also need to anchor these lofty thoughts into something more real. RS implies that societies must recognize their responsibilities towards all their dependent members, including non-human organisms, future generations, and the ecosystem as a whole. This view sits uneasily with the prevalent 'ethics' of the market, as markets are places in which numerous costs are externalized and so drop out (see Chapters 3 and 7). Importantly, non-market exchanges and other important interactions and relationships between individuals become invisible and are treated as valueless (when they ought to be valued, as these are what define us). Ironically, without such interactions there would be no markets, as relationships are crucial to sustaining market activity through, for example, maintenance and reproduction of the species, or the formation of interpersonal trust and shared aspirations. The invisibility of non-market interactions leads to a devaluation of caring relations, and of persons, animals and places for their own sake, and so social ties (other than those of market exchange) disappear from view. Those who have little or no market power, namely those with little or no wealth, thus have their perspectives and concerns overlooked (Held, 2006).

One immediate way to make 'ethics matter' is to render our relationships more visible, more present. RS therefore proposes a re-valuation of interdependency, affect and cooperation as central, inspired by feminist or relational *care ethics* which hold that interpersonal relationships and care are central to moral action as well as to individual and social wellbeing (Kerr et al, 2018). Universal standards, such as fairness, autonomy and impartiality found in the dominant consequentialist theories are important, but provide insufficient moral guidance, as they lay out abstractly *what is just* without considering *how to respond* (Gilligan, 1995). As Virginia Held argues in *The Ethics of Care* (2006), such theories typically view problems as a conflict of rights between egocentric, self-sufficient individuals. They foreground hypothetical moral rights and obligations without considering the specific situations in which problems emerge and without acknowledging how such problems elicit different – often unique – responses. Taking issue with this detached, atomistic view of people as self-interested individuals, Held proposes the metaphor of the *mothering person* as an alternative model for contemporary ethics. The relationship between mother and child demands cooperation, connection, listening, trust and intimacy. Although people in various situations and cultures frequently demonstrate such virtues by connecting with others (not just mothers or children), this is too often overlooked or its importance dismissed in the more liberal, rights-based, individualistic views of ethics.

Held's metaphor is a useful starting point to begin re-imagining ethics as being about more than justice in the abstract. Although it reinforces the stereotype of care as a feminine quality and overlooks conflict and disconnection (Sevenhuijsen, 2003), it also stresses that relationships are central to ethical reasoning, and that acknowledging specific relationships is key to how we organize (or re-organize) society, of which innovation is only part. It is thus crucial that we care for (not just about) the real interests of stakeholders – individuals and groups – to allow us to develop more mutually gratifying responses to different situations and needs.

These considerations are relevant to the responsible governance of new and emerging technologies, and thus to RI and RS, but they are also relevant to the subject of governance in general, whether that be of innovation systems or nation-states. Emergent technologies with unpredictable qualities, such as nanotechnologies and artificial intelligence, are often regulated by assessment approaches designed to provide an objective cost-benefit analysis of risk, irrespective of context or relationships. As these approaches forsake questions about how 'risk' is constructed, by whom and why, they overlook situational factors, dependence and power in STI processes. This is not an isolated occurrence, but rather reflects the salience (or lack thereof) of 'care' in the overall political economy in which the process in question is embedded.

The case of GMO in Europe provides a timely illustration of how market-driven innovations can fail when social, ethical and environmental concerns are not considered worthy of care. Framing resistance as stemming either from ignorance or a general rejection of science and progress (as discussed in Chapter 2) ignores the real issues GM presents for social relations through the shift to industrial agriculture, increased use of already-controversial pesticides and legal actions against small-hold farmers by behemoth corporations holding GM patents, who require the purchase of new seed every year. It is an example of how innovation processes elicit situated, context-dependent responses that defy market logic – even where GM seeds might indeed increase yields, many farmers have refused to use them for these reasons, which have nothing to do with fear of genetic modification itself (Gilbert, 2013).

It is worth speculating what the world might look like now if, rather than rushing towards commercialization of GMO, we had instead responsibly stagnated; if we had shown restraint, made ethics really matter and asked if the agricultural model in which GM was embedded really would allow us to live more gently, both with our natural environment and with those around us. In other words, by governing GM technology with care, taking more time to hear the European public's concerns, particularly their worries about the power of transnational firms in increasingly globalized markets, contamination of adjacent fields, and the threat to soil composition and biodiversity which large monoculture farms present (Legge Jr. and Durant, 2010), we may have found better ways to reap GM's potential for pest resistance, food production in arid areas, vitamin fortification and other potential benefits.

However, re-imagining how a more caring effort at public engagement might have reshaped the GM sector into something more acceptable to Europeans is not the only answer. Another option would have been for the EU simply not to invest in a form of innovation the public clearly didn't want, or at least, not yet. Perhaps other kinds of GMOs would eventually have been developed. Perhaps more time would have been spent on regulating how the innovators were acting, rather than assuming the market would allocate risk and benefit appropriately. And perhaps, if the EU had not invested so much in GM's promise of GDP growth (which never materialized), those resources, from research funds to advertising costs, would not have been lost; they could instead have been spent on other, more acceptable, measures to improve the production of food.

A responsible stagnation lens for viewing society and science

Drawing on an illustration from agricultural biotechnology in Europe helps illuminate the values of 'slowed reasoning' in STI and of precaution. These in turn open onto considerations that emphasize the importance of power imbalances, affect, care and relationships in STI governance, underlying the importance of questions such as: whom does innovation benefit? Is this innovation constitutive of nurturing relationships? How can innovation contribute to social wellbeing and to supporting the Earth's ecosystem? We embed these questions in a normative structure, which holds that relationships underpinned by care, whether interpersonal relationships or beyond (such as the relationship with our environment) are central to moral action.

However, governing innovation with care requires more than goodwill; as with RI, it requires education to empower wide participation. These challenges confer a responsibility on policy makers, researchers, industry players and other powerful actors to proactively engage with wider publics on more than just the technological output, but also to examine the underlying assumptions and aspirations, the socio-technical imaginary it is meant to serve. Here, RS goes further than RI, which tends to black-box questions about the 'politics of participation'; that is, about how participation is constituted and contested (see Chapter 2). Whereas the RI paradigm assumes that participatory processes will invariably generate better policies and better policymaking for 'all stakeholders', RS calls specific critical attention to the *hows, whos, whys,* and *wherefores* of participation-in-action. How do actors 'co-create' outcomes? How do they deliberate, and who gets invited to the deliberation? How do existing discourses, tools and institutional arrangements enable or constrain responsibility in STI? Does the choice to slow down or abandon an innovation process meaningfully exist? RS takes these questions as an important entry point to probe the rationalities of participation, which comprise conflict, politics and power, even within commitments to sharing and dialogue (Flyvbjerg, 1998). In this way, RS *politicizes* the ostensibly non-political concepts of 'responsibility' and 'innovation' found in RI, and foregrounds the political dimensions of moral reasoning and ethics in the innovation process.

RI calls for wide engagement before and during (rather than after) technologies are developed and brought to market, so as to allow more room for debate on the values, visions and commitments that inform STI decision-making, and more thoughtful consideration of research developments (Macnaghten et al, 2015). RS also calls for this, but advocates going one step further: to take an a-growth approach which allows deeper engagement with the underlying values the innovation serves, in particular the economic assumptions that go into valuing, desiring and pursuing that line of research. Therefore, ecological economics, political ecology, care ethics and critical perspectives on participation nurture our thinking about RS. By emphasizing dependency, power, politics and structure in innovation processes, and by asking whether these processes enable more caring relationships and innovation, we become more able to challenge dominant growth imperatives. As such, they serve as valuable sources of inspiration to guide and develop alternative innovation imaginaries and practices. However, each perspective in itself is insufficient to responsibly tackle the complexity of global problems. If ethics and policy frameworks are to work in the real world, they will need to be sufficiently flexible to incorporate a multitude of contrasting and sometimes conflicting perspectives, including anthropocentric and econo-centric values, ecological constraints, consequentialism and rights-based ethics, stagnation and productivity, collaboration and disruption. Embracing and working with diversity and pluralism is imperative both from a concern with democratic legitimacy and to ensure RS's practical applicability.

RS should therefore not be taken as a simplistic, hegemonic, one-size-fits-all approach, and certainly not something to be exported globally without due consideration for the power relations it itself presumes, and what kinds of practices it might unknowingly perpetuate in certain contexts. Instead, it should be seen as something (but not everything) that happens within the Fourth Quadrant, a critical-reflexive space within which it becomes possible and productive to juxtapose, challenge, try out and rethink novel problem-solving approaches to innovation, even RI and RS itself. This space allows us to reflectively consider the strengths and limitations of the different economic and ethical infrastructures at play, and to take the time to consider how different ideas can be combined, or at least positioned in such a way as to fruitfully inform, rather than impede, one another.

For the moment, we end with this: innovation should not only be seen as a science- and technology-driven endeavour designed to generate economic wealth, but as a more encompassing process by which novelty is taken up and circulated. Not-for-market social innovations are innovations too (see Chapter 5). In fact, arguing for slowed reasoning and responsible stagnation, if this can enable more socially responsive and environmentally friendly ways of doing things, is no less a form of innovation than the undirected 'creative destruction' (Schumpeter, 1942) championed by orthodox economics.

The question for our knight Innovation then, is not so much whether tilting at the windmills of the market will be profitable, but if it will be socially useful and sustainable over time. In this sense, RS offers a new lens for viewing the relationship between society and science, research, technology, and innovation. This includes slowing down the reflective decision-making process so that stakeholders (including the public at large), researchers and innovators may develop an a-growth perspective which considers the strengths, limitations and risks of a proposed innovation pathway as a collective, including how it will interact with the political economy of the real world. This is what the rest of Part III will explore.

5

Innovation for Social Needs

Effie Amanatidou, with George Gritzas

In the framework of responsible stagnation (RS), innovation is defined more broadly than bringing new or improved goods to the market or as the major means to increase productivity and growth following the Schumpeterian tradition.[1] This means that innovations can take place within the market or they may directly challenge the market by promoting RS in consumption, in this case by encouraging people *not* to buy new goods but to try to develop other ways to meet their needs. In this sense, innovation is not pursued for its own sake, and is not primarily targeting economic growth. Nor is it only a science- and technology-driven endeavour, but rather it is oriented primarily at addressing societal problems using the best possible means, some of which may not involve technological solutions at all.

At the same time, responsibility in RS also reflects the value of engaging the public in science, technology and innovation (STI), as in other responsible innovation (RI) frameworks. Because innovation in RS is seen as inclusive and participatory regardless of purpose, it can even seek to give voice and power to those with no market shares, while at the same time being socially, environmentally and ethically more responsible. Thus, as previously argued, RS can be thought of as a further innovation on the RI frameworks which have arisen in the context of the failure of globalized free-markets to adequately address social needs.

Several innovation types already exist that encompass some of the a-growth orientation of RS. Take for example the 'one laptop per child (OLPC)' project. The OLPC project is a non-profit initiative that was initiated by Nicholas Negroponte of Massachusetts Institute of Technology (MIT) Media Lab in 2005.[2] The main aim was to transform education by enabling children in low-income countries to have access to content, media and computer-programming environments at affordable costs, thus bringing them into equity with the tools available to pupils in richer countries. Although the OLPC project has been criticized in terms of cost-efficiency, low focus on maintainability and training, and has had limited success thus far, it has also been praised for inspiring later variants of low-cost, low-power laptops such as Eee PCs and Chromebooks, for making computer literacy a basic part of education globally, and for creating interfaces that work in any language.

Another example is the Nokia 1100, a mobile phone which had few features other than voice-calls and text-messaging, and was designed for developing countries. With sales of more than 200 million units within four years of its launch, the Nokia 1100 became one of the best-selling phones of all time (Virki, 2007), and is still in demand in resale markets across the world. Cheap phones like the Nokia 1100 also enabled other innovations, such as Safaricom's M-Pesa in Kenya, a text message-based banking service which allows people to send and receive money using their mobile phones, particularly valuable in countries whose rural economies depend on remittances from relatives working in urban centres or abroad.[3]

These are examples of so-called 'frugal innovations', which try to cover social needs in resource-constrained environments. They do this by reducing the complexity and cost of goods and their production in order to enable access by the poor. However, less expensive solutions created in the so-called developed and post-developed world to serve the needs of overlooked consumers in developing countries are not the only examples of frugal innovation. Several examples prove that the opposite is also possible, that is, frugal innovations created in the so-called developing world can also find a market in richer countries. In 1996 the Chinese firm Haier developed a washing machine called the Mini Magical Child that was designed for small daily loads and offered a real alternative to large, expensive washing machines. Another Chinese firm, Galanz, developed a low-cost, energy-efficient microwave small enough to fit inside small Chinese kitchens. Both the Haier washing machine and the Galanz microwave are currently being sold in the US and Europe (Zeschky et al, 2015). These show that there is a market for frugal innovations in post-industrial countries as well, naturally consisting of the poorer societal cohorts which are increasing in the context of slow economic growth and rising inequalities.

However, frugal innovation has been heavily criticized regarding underlying motivations and values as it is inherently embedded in a for-profit structure, and while such innovations might deliver benefits to the poor, this is not the driving incentive. Moreover, frugal innovation may replace traditional knowledge and restructure power relations (Pansera and Owen, 2018c), not necessarily to the benefit of the disadvantaged. For example, the business model enabled by M-PESA, of borrowing money in the morning to purchase goods to sell in the hope of paying off the loan in the evening with some profit, is not unproblematic. Frugal innovation is often based on the false assumption that resource scarcity is a natural condition in the Global South, rather than one that can be socially constructed to deny certain social sectors access to resources, and it avoids addressing poverty as a socio-economic problem that primarily requires a search for political, rather than technological, solutions (Pansera, 2018). In a similar vein, the notion of 'inclusive innovation' can be shaped by the values, normative worldviews and economic interests of those who advocate it, leveraging the rhetoric of inclusion in order to privilege Western-style market-oriented approaches and thus reinforcing the status quo (Pansera and Owen, 2018c). As will be further addressed in Chapter 6, the proliferation of fancy buzzwords such as frugal, reverse, Jugaad and so on imply a cross-pollination between the discourses of innovation and development that privileges 'technical fixes' which are disconnected from the particular social, cultural, environmental and political context of the place in question.

Social innovation: cutting across growth and stagnation

Whereas frugal innovation underlines low-cost production in ensuring wide accessibility under sometimes questionable motivations and effectiveness, social innovation tends to highlight public engagement and alternative ways of covering social needs which are not necessarily high-tech and not necessarily market-driven (Grimm et al, 2013). Edwards-Schachter and Wallace (2017) distinguish several waves of different understandings of 'social innovation', starting with Drucker's (1957) work on post-modernity where social innovation was linked to a search for organizational efficiency through other than technological means. Between the 1970s and the 1980s, however, the term was used to define products, processes and services mediated by technologies but created for social purposes, defined as 'survival problems' like environmental degradation, racism and population regulation. This happened alongside another perception of social innovation that possibly reflected the proliferation of third sector initiatives and social movements as providers of services in sectors such as healthcare, employment and education in the 1980s. By the start of the 21st century, social innovation began to be used to label practices of third sector organizations while also representing activities of social enterprises and emerging corporate social responsibility (CSR) initiatives (Mumford, 2002), thus putting the business world back into the social innovation landscape alongside the third sector (although not without criticizing the profit-making motivations of the private sector).

Although a common definition of the concept does not really exist today, a definition widely used within the policy cycles of the EU institutions is that: 'Social innovations are new ideas that meet social needs, create social relationships and form new collaborations. These innovations can be products, services or models addressing unmet needs more effectively' (EC, 2019b).

This coheres with the underlying values of RS, which sees social innovation as a way of satisfying social needs with sustainable and accessible solutions which are not necessarily market-driven (though it does not preclude this). The Jaipur

Foot, a $45 ultramodern prosthetic developed by an Indian non-profit, which rivals the lightness and flexibility of a $12,000 prosthetic produced in the US, would be such a case.[4] However, RS also supports the proposition that 'innovation' is not restricted to technology. New configurations of social relations, for example the creation of civil partnership in the UK as a new institution for same-sex couples who were (at the time) not legally able to marry, would also be considered as a social innovation.

For the purposes of this discussion, however, we will mainly concentrate on innovation which has a material aspect. The type of innovation Amanatidou and colleagues (2018) have called 'Society in Control', where society plays a key role in the innovation cycle, from initiation to diffusion and delivery, has a lot in common with RI. But this form of social innovation is also aimed at transformation based on shared values of social engagement and democracy-based decision-making, empowerment of citizens and stakeholders, social justice, solidarity, a good society and social cohesion (Etzioni, 2004). These values overtake growth and profit-making motives. Moulaert and colleagues (2005) also stress the importance of the empowerment dimension in social innovations and the increasing level of participation of all – but especially of deprived – stakeholder groups. This can also include what Seyfang and Smith (2007, p 585) have called grassroots innovations, or 'innovative networks of activists and organizations that lead bottom-up solutions for sustainable development; solutions that respond to the local situation and the interests and values of the communities involved'. Grassroots innovations are driven by two key goals: firstly, to satisfy social needs of people or communities who may in some way be disadvantaged by or excluded from the mainstream market economy, through helping to develop their capacities; and second, by an ideological commitment to develop alternatives to hegemonic regimes, which includes re-ordering the values and indicators of success for initiatives.

'Society in Control' social innovations reflect much more than the broader institutional shift towards public inclusion in science and towards openness that was discussed in Chapter 2. They are not just about enabling society's participation in the research and innovation cycle, nor are they 'engagements' to ensure social acceptance of new technologies or increase public trust. Such innovations are actually guided and implemented with society being in the driving seat. The role of society is not limited to that of being consulted or even to that of co-creator or co-producer of solutions to societal challenges; it is upgraded to the higher scale in Arnstein's (1969) 'ladder of citizen participation', that is, to being in control, a key agent of social transformation. Although we do not say that RS *is* or *must be* a Society in Control innovation, the dominance of social values such as justice, solidarity and cohesion over economic benefits for the few, and the focus on alternative solutions to 'sustainable development' means that this type of innovation fits comfortably into what we have called the Fourth Quadrant of the innovation matrix, an idea worthy of further exploration.

Society in Control: social innovation for responsible stagnation

As noted earlier, Society in Control innovations are usually placed outside the market as they tend to be underlined by non-monetary transactions, collective self-governance, informal types of organization and democratic decision-making procedures. They are seen by many as ventures within the social and solidarity economy.

Before we continue, however, we do want to draw attention to a distinction in the way the Western world (or Global North) sees the social and solidarity economy compared to how it is seen the Global South. Interestingly, there is a difference in aspirations. In the Global North, which we define as those nations where the liberal, capitalist economy is well established, the 'social economy' is perceived as complementary to the mainstream economy. The social economy primarily addresses the needs of society that the state does not cover sufficiently or at all and/or the private sector sees no profit in covering (Murray et al, 2010). By contrast, the Global South perspective is developing this concept as a force for social change, the bearer of a project for an alternative society to neoliberal globalization (Boulianne et al, 2003). The world economy is pluralistic at the local level, ranging from profit-making motivations and market-based economies, to motivations highlighting social over private benefits, to non-monetary transactions, much of which is not measured by Gross Domestic Product (GDP) (Gibson-Graham, 2010). It follows, therefore, that RI discourses must be enriched to encompass all, that is, both conventional and alternative innovation and economic theories and practices. This is where widening the context of 'responsible' by cutting across the stagnation and innovation quadrants becomes relevant. At the same time, as we argued in Chapter 4, there is a need to re-formulate responsibility to incorporate a 'commitment to care' that is, to adopt an ethico-political obligation to bring the perspectives of the marginalized and the invisible to the fore. We will return to these ideas in more detail in Chapter 6, where the very concept of 'development' and its underlying assumptions and values are critically examined.

Lack of acknowledgement of the pluralism of values and economies means that social innovations of the Society in Control type are usually overlooked in mainstream innovation analysis and policy discourses as they are not market-driven innovations. Some hardcore innovation scholars do not even see innovation features in these ventures. Although different types of innovation have long been acknowledged (organizational, governance innovations and so on), empirical innovation studies still focus predominantly on technological or business innovations in the manufacturing and service sectors. The Fourth Quadrant, however, offers space for their consideration due to the underlying a-growth orientation of RS, and the strong emphasis on social, ethical and environmental responsibilities and inclusive and deliberative approaches. In this regard, the concepts of social innovation and RS are mutually supporting each other. On the one hand, social innovations that place society in control accommodate slower decision-making processes which support the principles of living gently, restraint, making ethics matter and broadening of ideas, as a particular configuration of change which is central to RS. On the other hand, RS offers conceptual freedom from mainstream economics, with its associated growth obsession, to encompass other types of innovation that are embedded in society, even though they may be located outside of the transactional market. This offers a wider context for RI, allowing and motivating experimentation with innovation governance and also exploring a much wider part of reality in innovation practice.

Take for instance the challenge of addressing poverty in rural India. Mainstream rhetoric would call for economic growth based on national and foreign investments to increase the exploitation of natural resources and cheap labour, championing the consequent assumed creation of jobs (albeit these are most likely to be displaced from elsewhere in the global economy). RS enables an alternative way of thinking about how to create prosperity to improve people's lives without the ecological or social downside associated with exploitation. This could be through low-cost solutions which respect the environment, yet still provide access for poorer people to empower themselves. The Barefoot College,[5] for example, trains women in deprived areas (initially in India and now worldwide) as solar engineers, innovators and educators. Thus trained, they return to their communities to educate yet more women on how to address their energy needs. The solutions applied are renewable and infrastructure-independent (for example solar panels, photovoltaics) and incorporate recycled materials where possible. Barefoot College also appreciates and spreads the existing, but possibly forgotten, wisdom of the local elderly in various areas. For example, they teach the traditional and sustainable cultivation of land where modern high-intensity fertilizers and cultivation methods might prove totally ineffective or counter-productive. Thus, the social responsibility of Barefoot College goes beyond the empowerment of the poor to bridging generations and capitalizing on traditional knowledge and social capital that is usually overlooked when examining the actual resources of a place from an international, short-term profit perspective.

Another challenge is looking after the elderly as societies change in response to the ageing of populations and the shift of younger generations to cities in search of work. Whereas technological or medical solutions in this area are of crucial importance, and will have invaluable impact, other types of activities that lie in the social sphere, particularly strengthening the social connectedness of the isolated elderly, are also important, even though they may not be receiving as high attention. The GoodGym,[6] an award-winning social innovation, was set up in 2009 as a not-for-profit company in the UK to create a new model of voluntary action that combines physical exercise with doing good for the community. Runners from GoodGym stop off on their routes to carry out physical tasks for community organizations and to support isolated older people through social visits and help with one-off tasks they cannot do on their own. Similarly, the Foster Families programme in Russia, established across several regions since 2010, pairs older people with adoptive foster families who are responsible for providing care to them in a home environment as opposed to residential facilities (for example nursing homes). The establishment of the foster family relies on a tripartite agreement between the foster family, the older person and the Complex Centre of Social Service under the regional Ministry of Labour and Social Development. Another example is the Kajood handicraft community enterprise in Thailand, a community-based organization producing handicrafts made from Kajood, a plant material which grows in southern Thailand. The programme aims to contribute to older people's active ageing in the region through addressing the three core components of health, social participation and financial security. In 2006 the programme became a community enterprise, receiving funding and support from local government organizations. As a result of the income generated from selling the handicrafts, the programme is now considered financially self-sufficient.[7] Such relational initiatives are of increasing importance given the role of staying active and socially connected in the fight against dementia and Alzheimer's and helps to preserve older people's ability to remain in their own homes.

Other innovation areas include education, social inclusion and food security. The initiative for exchanging education for habitation ('Tausche Bildung für Wohnen') was developed in 2011 in Germany, aimed at achieving equal opportunities and social integration for urban children living in disadvantaged areas of Duisburg-Marxloh by offering young adults (mostly students) a true-to-life field of work in teaching, supporting and coaching disadvantaged children. As 'godparents' the students can live in these areas without paying rent, and in return they

educate and supervise local children. The Viennese initiative
iss mich! (eat me!), begun in 2014, aims to improve nutrition
and reduce food waste. It offers a catering and delivery service,
but collaborates with Caritas, a charity that helps unemployed,
young, single mothers find a job, so most of their employees are
part-time workers selected by social workers at Caritas welfare
houses.[8] Participants cook vegetables that cannot be marketed
into soups and stews. They also use natural methods to prolong
durability and distribute bio-certified food in the Vienna area.

While all of these examples are locally derived solutions, they
are also part of a more global configuration of change which
allows these types of innovation to spread through alternative
networks and fora which are dedicated to such ideals. Iss mich!,
for example, is part of the global 'eat, instead of throw away'
movement which aims to use food that would otherwise be
thrown away by supermarkets and restaurants to feed people in
homes, shelters and on the streets, or to make nutrition more
readily available to those on limited incomes. As noted earlier,
such innovations can serve both populations in countries which
cannot afford to provide such services, and those in richer
countries where inequality is increasing and governments have
chosen not to create or maintain social welfare programmes to
fill those needs.

Ethically responsible social innovations for responsible stagnation

Ethical responsibility is another major feature of RS. Maintaining
reasonable prices to provide access by the poor to basic products
is as much an aspect of ethical responsibility as is fighting child
labour or safeguarding fair prices for small producers in large
markets. Calvário and Kallis (2016) analyzed the case of 'no
intermediaries' food distribution networks that emerged in
Greece at the height of the debt crisis, which was occurring
at roughly the same time the EU's framework for Responsible
Research and Innovation (RRI) was being developed. The
main motivation was to provide access to basic nutritional needs
when many people in Greece suddenly found themselves unable
to feed their families. This was coupled with the intention to

prevent wholesalers from taking advantage of local producers and thus the 'no intermediaries' movement was born. These are volunteer-based groups that organize distributions where farmers sell their products directly to the public at pre-agreed prices. Consumers have access to quality products with prices 20–50 per cent lower than in retail markets, and farmers are paid on the spot, which is not the case when merchants mediate. Producers are selected according to quality, price and proximity, avoiding large footprints on the environment. Most of these groups also require farmers to give 2–5 per cent of their goods to impoverished families for free. In 2014 there were 45 no-middlemen groups, while 5,000 tonnes of food was distributed from 2012 to 2014. In December 2017 it was decided to set up a Panhellenic network of 'no intermediaries' with the aim of supporting producers and strengthening the direct distribution of Greek products at reasonable and fair prices, by coordinating all the self-organized 'no intermediaries' initiatives in Greece. We may note that the crisis in which many of the Southern eurozone states still find themselves illustrates the point that those whose prospects are destroyed by traditional Schumpeterian innovation are not necessarily those who benefit from the implied creation.

Market-based innovations may indeed serve important social needs, but the profit motive means that this often includes unethical production conditions, such as in the case of smartphone production using conflict minerals and illegal child labour. Although not precisely a Society in Control innovation, social enterprises such as Fairphone show that this does not necessarily need to be the case. Based in Amsterdam, Fairphone was founded to develop a mobile device that does not contain conflict minerals (which in smartphones are typically gold, tin, tantalum and tungsten), has fair labour conditions for the workforce along the supply chain producing it and employs a modular configuration that encourages people to extend the life of their phone by making the components easy to replace. Haucke (2018) notes that as a technical artefact the Fairphone also demonstrates the owner's support for a sustainable lifestyle (although it is admittedly an expensive purchase and therefore not pro-poor). While it has gone through a number of phases over the years and had a lot of ups and downs (Akemu et al, 2016), it has also had continued community support and success in crowdfunding, so much so that its second production run has recently sold out.[9] Needless to say, this kind of social innovation also exists within the framework of the wider Fair Trade movement that has been active for 60 years.[10]

Although some of these examples of social innovations are market-driven, their focus on ethical responsibility constrains profit-making motivations, while their emphasis on reducing waste and unnecessary consumption marks their attention to environmental responsibility. In short, the innovation process is informed throughout by the primary objective of taking responsibility for the entire value chain and its by-products, and seeking to use less to fill the same social need. Fairphone, and indeed the whole Fair Trade movement, makes a good example of how innovation *can* be aimed at the market, and *can* still generate profit and growth while demonstrating key aspects of RS.

A-growth social innovations for responsible stagnation

Being growth-agnostic does not mean an enterprise cannot grow, only that this is neither its prime objective nor a significant driver of its innovation processes. Still, as we will discuss in Chapter 7, it is easier to adopt an a-growth model within the broader field of social innovation because the demand for return of investment, if it exists at all, is different. The Jaipur Foot, for instance, is largely funded as a third sector organization, and it is not obliged to cover all its costs through sales, thus allowing the prosthetic to be given for free or sold at a very low price.

Social innovations can also be based on thoroughly non-monetary transactions which address basic social needs in a manner that actively promotes, even requires, public engagement. Timebanking is one such example, although not a recent one, as the idea of the 'time bank' was developed by Washington law professor Edgar Cahn in 1995.[11] Time banks bring people and local organizations together to help each other, utilizing previously untapped resources and skills, valuing work which is normally unrewarded and valuing people who find themselves marginalized from the conventional market economy (Seyfang, 2006). Time banks can be initiated by municipalities or organizations of the third sector (for example charities or foundations), but they can also be an initiative of citizens and social movements. Boyle (2005) argues that timebanking is closely linked to sustainable development due to its ability to measure and reward recycling and restrained consumption patterns, its orientation towards social inclusion and building individual and collective social capital and healthy communities and by recognizing assets which have real value in neighbourhoods, but no value in the market economy, such as good neighbours, or older people with a lifetime's skills and experience to share. Seyfang also considers time banks as tools to promote sustainable consumption. Apart from satisfying local needs with local resources through relational transactions, time banks are proof of the existence of alternative spaces of socio-economic transactions based on ethical values like mutuality, trust, equality and reciprocity. In this sense they valorize assets that are ignored in the market economy despite being important in the environmental and human ecosystems (Amanatidou et al, 2015).

Social innovations and the role of public policy

Social innovations that intend to bring social transformation may clash with the dominant institutional setting (Haxeltine et al, 2015). Established institutions may, for various reasons, place barriers to the diffusion of certain innovations. For instance, the movement of 'no intermediaries' that appeared in Greece during the financial crisis was beneficial for low-income families but not for traditional open-market intermediaries. The initiative was considered unethical competition and was banned in certain municipalities because it affected the vested interests of participants in long-established open markets where members paid regular taxes and thus enabled wealth redistribution (to some extent). Likewise, social innovations may assert the interests of certain social groups over those of others. In such cases social innovation might inadvertently promote social exclusion with some unintended or anti-social consequences. Like any other innovation, these too should be the subject of the kinds of deliberative procedures that characterize RI.

This is partly because the role that the state will eventually take vis-à-vis supporting social innovation is a political decision, with multiple stakeholders who may have conflicting needs and values. It may be the case that certain types of social innovations would not flourish in contexts where the state is the main provider of welfare services. However, it may also be that, in a time of austerity, or where the role of the state as a provider of welfare services is uncertain and/or led by short-term goals linked to political cycles, the low quality of public services may trigger the emergence of social innovations which can help people counter the effects of secular stagnation. In these cases emergent social innovations may be seen as a desirable buffer which can loosen the social sphere from its dependence on state agency, but it may also be seen as enabling neoliberal projects aimed at reducing the role of the state. The real challenges for social innovation may only arise when it threatens the profits of private sector, particularly multinational operators.

Drawing on three case studies, that is, the Social Technologies Network in Brazil, the Honey Bee Network and People's Science Movements in India, Fressoli and colleagues (2014) studied the encounters of grassroots innovation movements with established STI institutions. As they characteristically note, in their interactions with STI, grassroots movements face the challenge of having their goals captured and integrated into dominant agendas and/or of needing to mobilize resistance in order to transform mainstream systems of innovation and technological change. These dynamics are shaped by several factors, such as policy frameworks and policy culture, the level of community organization, forms of resistance to imposed technological conformity and the social innovators' capacity to generate interest among policy makers.

Overall, it is clear that regulation, relevant policies and incentives affect the adoption of social innovations either in a negative or a positive way, just as with any other type of innovation. In countries encouraging social entrepreneurship (for example Canada, Austria or the UK) social innovation has blossomed throughout the years, although certain national regulations may be hindering voluntary action, for example by job-seekers in fear of losing social benefits (Seyfang, 2003). Thus, even without providing direct taxpayer-funded support, policy makers can enable the social innovation sector in a number of other ways.

A case that is illustrative of the role played by governance, policy and institutions in spreading social innovations is the Quebec Model, which is characteristic of the convergence of the notion of 'path dependency' and that of 'path building' (capacity of actors to break the regulatory framework and to build another one). Providing an historical analysis, Klein and colleagues (2013) argue that the most important innovations shaping the Quebec Model occurred in three areas: governance, co-construction and co-production, and the economy. More specifically, social movements switched from demanding action from others to engaging themselves in developing proactive responses to social problems, enabling new ways of coordinating and regulating innovation that are underpinned by participatory governance, co-production of services or activities and co-construction of public policies. As part of this model, alternative modes of ownership and use of diverse resources emerged, thus introducing plurality into the economic landscape.

Aspiring to contribute to the EU policy debate on social innovation, the Social Innovation Community Project has identified five ways that public policy could support social innovations, which we think worthy of mention, although noting that we are still a long way from a well-developed field of 'social innovation policy'. This would include: a) funding for early-stage initiatives, scale-ups and intermediaries; b) supportive regulation and legal frameworks; c) opening up public procurement processes to social enterprises; d) using public assets in socially innovative ways; and e) raising awareness and building skills to enable people to make use of these opportunities (Gabriel, 2016). The TRANSIT project (TRANsformative Social Innovation Theory) has published a similar *Manifesto on Social Innovation*, calling on policy makers and politicians (among others) to commit to creating and supporting spaces for experimentation and learning, to be flexible and adaptive to changing societal demands and to engage with social innovators in a process to defend, nurture and improve necessary public institutions (Haxeltine et al, 2015).[12] The TRANSIT Manifesto also promotes 13 principles for innovation, among which are the need to experiment with and acknowledge alternative economic formulations, including the solidarity economy, social economy, social entrepreneurship, green economy, degrowth, sharing economy, circular economy, and others which (although not formulated by them as such) take an a-growth approach.

Reality shows that certain social innovation initiatives and movements share a great deal with the values of RS discussed in Chapter 4. Including the Fourth Quadrant into our thinking offers the conceptual freedom from the growth obsession to allow innovation to also encompass types that are embedded in society, even though they may be located outside of the market. Although they are usually overlooked by mainstream economic and innovation theories these kinds of innovations address societal needs in sustainable, socially, ethically and environmentally responsible ways and prioritize giving a key role to society in a range of formats beyond the usual structures of 'public engagement'. Considering these as vital to understandings of both RI and RS may help make them visible and more viable, by convincing policy makers to create initiatives which can support a wider range of innovation as a way of maintaining prosperity without GDP-measured growth.

Unfortunately, most of the social innovations in globally integrated post-industrial nations are still devised to serve the dominant economic growth paradigm by complementing the role of the state and the market, although a few of them do aspire to bring wider societal change following post-development philosophies such as de-growth or a-growth. On the contrary, the Global South is characterized by more ambitious ventures of social innovations that not only sideline the global market economy but can also provide the 'developed world' with valuable experience if we want to take RS pathways. In the next chapter, we explore how RS might be understood in that context by looking through the lens of care.

6

The Plurality of Technology and Innovation in the Global South

Mario Pansera, with Keren Naa Abeka Arthur,
Andrea Jimenez and Poonam Pandey

At face value, responsible innovation (RI) and Responsible Research and Innovation (RRI) address several aspects which were neglected in previous innovation concepts. With a more holistic framework, they suggest a great potential for global adaptability. However, a purely optimistic view risks ignoring the role that technological innovation has had in the so-called developing world and perpetuating patterns that conflict with the 'ethics matters' and 'living gently' aspects of responsible stagnation (RS). As mentioned in Chapter 5, the Global South represents a great reservoir of alternative ways of framing innovation. While these do not consciously conceptualize themselves as RS, they do open up new ways of thinking about technical change beyond the fetishism of endless growth – ideas which form an essential part of the Fourth Quadrant of the innovation matrix. This chapter highlights the complexity and challenges of innovation in the Global South, drawing on the reflections of anthropologists and post-colonial scholars to consider how responsibility (beyond growth) and RI might be approached to make these concepts relevant to countries in the Global South, without repeating the patterns of colonization which are contrary to RS's underlying ethos of care.

In *The World and the West*, the British historian Arnold J. Toynbee reflects on the role of technology as a transformative social agent within foreign societies. He anticipated what the field of Science and Technology Studies (STS) would eventually come to claim – that technology (and therefore innovation) is culturally, socially and politically constructed, whether unconsciously or by design:[1]

> Technology operates on the surface of life, and therefore it seems practicable to adopt a foreign technology without putting oneself in danger of ceasing to be able to call one's soul one's own. [… however,] if one abandons one's own traditional technology and adopts a foreign technology instead, the effect of this change on the technological surface of life will not remain confined to the surface, but will gradually work its way down to the depths till the whole of one's traditional culture has been undermined and the whole of the foreign culture has been given entry. (Toynbee, 1953, p 55)

With these words, Toynbee suggests that importing technology does not merely mean transferring technical and scientific know-how. It also implies the absorption (often in a traumatic manner) of ways of living and being. This reflection is of fundamental importance for those within the so-called developing world who must ask 'what would this technology be for in our society, our cultural context, our villages, our cities?' Toynbee's intuitions beg an even more crucial question: 'what kind of (social, cultural and economic) transformations do non-Western societies need to catch up with the so-called developed world?' For example, we might question whether such transformation is inclusive or exclusive, and whether it is legitimate, desirable, fair and responsible. We might also question who would be allowed to answer such questions and through what mechanisms, and what they stand to gain and lose by the introduction of a foreign innovation.

This debate is intrinsically connected with the role played, and the impact on human societies produced, by technological development and innovation. There is an increasing consensus around the idea that technology has to emerge from, and be governed by, a socio-political framework which privileges responsibility as a key anchor point and social norm (Owen et al, 2013a). But it is not clear what responsibility means in the social construction of technological futures. From a layperson's perspective, being responsible is positive while irresponsibility carries with it a negative connotation. Thus, the ability of any society to ensure responsible behaviour can be seen as a good thing that many encourage, or at least find difficult to oppose. Despite this, the concepts of RI and RRI[2] that have recently emerged in science, technology and innovation (STI) policy across Europe, the US and elsewhere, continue to be contested. Critics of RI would agree that the objectives are, in themselves, creditable. Nevertheless, concerns are raised around issues such as what constitutes RI globally, how can this be fostered and how can these ideas be applied to contexts which are varied in terms of sector (Asante et al, 2014) and geographic location (de Hoop et al, 2016; Vasen, 2017).

A key theme in this critique is the potential incompatibility of RI with non-Western settings or those in the Global South. The Global North nations benefit from a first-mover advantage vis-à-vis the rest of the world, allowing them to dictate the terms of globalization to the South. Note, however, that following the Global Financial Crisis of 2008, the terms of political power are now shifting, with the result that policies of the supposedly developed nations are increasingly being dictated by, and their resources owned by, rising industrial and political powers such as China and India.

This chapter focuses on three connected points. The first reflects on the discourse of innovation, where and how it originated, its evolution and its political dimensions across relationships between the Global North and the Global South. The main argument on which these strands of research seem to converge is the idea that the 'discourse of development' has been used (at least by some powerful groups) as a post-colonial tool of control. More recently we have also witnessed an increasing use of the word 'innovation' in the broader discourse of development that reflects a shift from a state-driven narrative of development to a private-driven narrative of global capitalism. As a result, from the 1980s, the discourse of development has been cross-pollinated with discourses focussed on technological progress, efficiency and market-driven innovation.

The second point, as described in detail in Chapter 2, stems from the fact that the notions of RI and RRI are born in the West and are shaped on Western history, institutions and cultural settings. We examine to what extent this way of framing responsibility is exportable to non-Western environments. Similarly, we consider to what extent the dynamics of democratic participation, public engagement, reflexivity and all the elements that characterize responsibility in STI policy can be adapted or transferred to other situations with different traditions and practices of deliberation. This is particularly relevant for a world in which the impact of techno-scientific innovation transcends national borders.

The third point is a direct consequence of the first two: non-Western contexts have a rich diversity of local cultures with their own ways of making sense of the world, and of creating and using knowledge. Therefore, 'responsibility' needs to be reformulated to address and protect such diversity. We suggest, moreover, that the vulnerable in the developed world are no less in danger of losing their communities and culture in the face of increasing globalized homogeneity, if market-based technologies and policies converge to that small set which will maximize international corporate profitability.

From discourse of development to politics of innovation

There is a direct relationship between the expansion of knowledge, the expansion of trade and the expansion of empire. That relationship continues, although in the reframed discourse of globalization it is referred to as the relationship between the expansion of technology/information, the expansion of economic opportunities and the expansion of 'the market' (Tuhiwai-Smith, 2002). First, post-colonial and (more recently) post-development scholars have argued that the idea of progress, framed in terms of technological advances, has been used since the industrial revolution and the rise of capitalism (from the 17th century on) by imperial powers as a means to dominate and control the conquered (the dispossessed populations in their own countries and what is now known as the Global South). The colonial imposition on countries in the Global South not only meant the Northern elite's appropriation of territories and exploitation of people, but also involved the disruption of local trades, the imposition of foreign knowledge/languages and the subordination of indigenous peoples' knowledge. This process, referred to in the literature as 'epistemic violence' (Spivak, 1994), was key to the process of colonization, just as much as was the expansion of trade and exploitation of resources. Teo (2010, p 298) notes this process exists even today and happens when 'theoretical interpretations regarding empirical results implicitly or explicitly construct the *Other* as inferior or problematic, despite the fact that alternative interpretations, equally viable based on the data, are available' (emphasis in original). This process of undermining traditional and non-Western methods and bodies of knowledge was at the heart of the colonial project, and technology has played a key role (Harding, 2011).

The coupling of industrial technology with economic growth has been central to the reshaping and remaking of modern Western societies. This techno-economic paradigm entered the non-Western world in the form of promises and persuasions that early colonizers brought in to improve trade and production of tradable goods (Arnold, 2013; Prakash, 1999). Eventually, modern Western technology became a tool of capitalist domination and control. In the colonial regime, domestic technology and knowledge systems were systematically undermined, while Western technology was promoted and transferred to the colonies in order to maintain competitive advantages and knowledge asymmetry. The season of colonial emancipation, after World War II, marks the beginning of a new world order but also a different way of framing the use of technological progress as a tool of domination (Marcuse, 1966).

This shift was characterized by the promotion of the 'discourse of development' – a powerful buzzword (Rist, 2007) – as a new dominant narrative to continue the exploitation of the vulnerable by non-military means, for example, by technological and institutional transfer.

The Western project of development began in earnest after World War II. Since then, ideas of technology transfer from the developed to the developing world started to be a feature of the development discourse, famously embodied in the inaugural address on 20 January 1949 by the President of the United States, Harry Truman, in his proclamation 'to make available to peace-loving peoples the benefits of our store of technical knowledge in order to help them realize their aspirations for a better life' (Truman, 1964). Domestically, in newly independent nations such as India, the ideals of Western S&T-led development and progress were fully embraced and adopted by the educated and political elites who were significantly influenced by Western education systems (Visvanathan, 1988). The privileging of Western S&T-led development through state-sponsored, top-down and centrally controlled programmes such as construction of large dams and modernization of agriculture resulted in multiple tensions and conflicts that, contrary to Truman's vision (but in accordance with the history of industrialized production) led to destruction, displacement of local populations and violence (Shiva, 1991). How could it have been expected to be otherwise when, in the absence of countervailing power such as regulation and unionization, the history of industrial 'progress' was marked by the dispossession of the vulnerable even in the so-called developed nations?

However, since the 1970s this project has witnessed a progressive shift in emphasis and delivery. A macroeconomic focus based largely on donor-led, institution-building initiatives, often involving state-funded finance and technology transfer from North to South, gave way to a more granular approach directed towards local, situated interventions (Escobar, 2012), often involving a wider range of funding sources (such as private foundations and companies) and stakeholders (such as Non-Governmental Organizations (NGOs), local communities and social enterprises). Towards the end of the 1970s the discontents of development, fuelled by evidence of ecological destruction, technological controversies and rising inequalities, resulted in people's movements all over the world. In the Western world, owning to economic downturns between the 1970s and the 1980s, themselves triggered by resource constraints, particularly in fossil fuels, the public debate about technology was being reframed into innovation systems approaches, making innovation a key ingredient in addressing the challenges of declining economic growth (Freeman, 1987; Martin, 2012).

In the non-Western world, however, it was not until the end of the 1990s that the highly politicized and criticized 'discourse of development' – which had begun to highlight inequality, injustice and economic and political violence – was reframed as a neutral discourse of innovation in science and industrial policies. These ideas were promoted by international organizations and nation-states but also by an increasing number of management and business scholars.[3] Eventually, not only has innovation been sold as a magic formula for growth, it has also been promoted as a panacea for 'inclusion' and 'equality' – for example by notions of inclusive growth and inclusive innovation (Pansera and Owen, 2018a) and more recently 'social innovation' (see Chapter 5), although it is more widely recognised now that the market will not 'trickle down' affluence without appropriate regulation and redistribution.

In the same period, the topics of development and poverty, once dominated by development economists, had gone under the radar of management, organization and innovation scholars (Kolk et al, 2013). As a result of reflections on the limits of Western models of innovation (mostly the 'systems of innovation' approach), a huge variety of terms – some old like 'appropriate technology', and some new, like 'resource-constrained innovation (RCI)' – began to populate the business and management literature. Buzzwords such as frugal, reverse, Jugaad, Bottom of the Pyramid (BOP), Gandhian, empathetic and 'pro-poor versus from-the-poor' have recently been attached to 'innovation', attracting the attention of heterogeneous communities of scholars around the world (Pansera and Owen, 2018c). This proliferation of buzzwords suggests, at least in academic publications, a cross-pollination between the discourses of development and innovation (Pansera and Owen, 2018a). The literature shows that this cross-pollination privileges technical fixes while simultaneously a-politicizing (or depoliticizing) the notion of development. In other words, poverty and social exclusion tend to be framed as technical issues to be solved through the implementation of new technologies, rather than addressed by a process of political transformation.

Locating this within a market paradigm disconnects it from the social, cultural, environmental and political, particularly in relation to poverty and social exclusion, financial and material scarcity and political instability, while the concept of 'inclusive growth' remains vague and heterogeneous. Inclusiveness in general advocates for more equal and fair distribution, with the underlying theme being that the poor are excluded from the benefits of development and consequently need to be included in those productive activities that create economic growth (Peredo, 2012). What is less clear, however, is how this supposed growth is to be shifted from 'exclusive' to 'inclusive'.

In this context, the rise of the global neoliberal ideology in the 1980s was an important moment. While the meaning of the term 'neoliberalism' is much contested, we use it here in the sense of the application of policies proposed by the so-called Washington Consensus, which imposed a policy of 'structural adjustment', including liberalization of trade, removal of tariff barriers, the privatization of several sectors of national economies and the promotion of the 'small' state – that is, a state which concerns itself primarily with maintenance of the rule of law and the rights of ownership and exploitation. This form of neoliberalism promoted (so-called) free globalized markets, arguing that development should be a spontaneous phenomenon, occurring most effectively when the endogenous (internal), productive forces of society are coordinated through market forces. Catalyzed by Western nations (notably the US and the EU) and multilateral institutions such as the International Monetary Fund (IMF), World Bank and World Trade Organization (WTO), the neoliberal turn radically changed the way development interventions were framed and delivered. It also opened the door for business and management scholars to treat development as a legitimate object of study. Innovation, therefore, has grown to become a seemingly indispensable element of development policy and practice in the 21st century.[4] But innovation in this setting is largely an elite project which has been transferred to 'others', including the dispossessed in Western nations: people living in poverty, women, immigrants and other social minorities that are excluded from mainstream society.

Not surprisingly, RI and RRI emerged also in the West, thus causing us to question whether its exportation is necessary or beneficial. These notions assume that innovation promises benefits that can help nations grow economically for the wellbeing of their inhabitants. It champions an outcome and process-based approach to justifying innovations and although its discourse is vague on the specifics of what should characterize innovations to be considered useful, it emphasizes the principles of 'care for the future' and using appropriate processes (particularly in the RI formulation described by Stilgoe et al, 2013). This links closely with the notion of inclusivity which dominates the innovation for development literature (Pansera and Martinez, 2017). Thus, RI and RRI appear to adopt a much broader and interpretively flexible innovation approach.

However, even if there have been success stories that have emerged from using this approach to foster responsibility in innovation experiences, we have to be cautious of the fact that what has worked for one may not work for another, and that the argument that underdevelopment is a result of failure to adopt an innovation that has worked successfully for another (or innovation in general) is flawed. On the other hand, it is certainly true that there may be aspects of already existing innovation models, and by extension, RI and RRI frameworks, that could be adapted in beneficial ways, considering the fact that many of the same issues that 'irresponsible innovation' poses in the North are valid in the South (in particular externalizing costs, as discussed in Chapters 3 and 7), and have global implications that go beyond national borders. But in our view, it would be an error to think that such a 'transfer' can occur smoothly, without frictions and conflicts or without winners and losers.

The fundamental issue is that RI and RRI (but also RS as framed in this book) posit a sort of universalistic 'global' conception of responsibility. This is problematic because there are at least two ways in which 'global' can be understood. The first conceptualization holds that global is generally first local of some place, yet becomes hegemonic through power, persuasion and resources; it grows from the specific into the universal, and from the diverse into the homogeneous. The processes by which this 'universal global' takes form often end up excluding and destroying certain ways of knowing, innovating and being. Human geographers, for example Doreen Massey (2005), have argued that what is 'global' is always local from somewhere, but it adopts a universal form due to uneven relations of power. In this sense, the economic forces that concentrate most of the power also construct what is understood to be good or desirable, creating hegemonic stories that seem to be the norm. The possibility to create new hegemonic narratives is not something that is available to all because power is structurally differentiated. This affects the current understanding of globalization and the form it has taken, which is part of a unified discourse so imbued in our understanding of the world that it is almost impossible to imagine alternative ways to it. However, this particular type/ form of globalization does not exist arbitrarily but is in fact a project shaped by people in power who have institutionalized it through different organizations, governments and discourses which have inevitably prioritized Western knowledge and subordinated that of others.

The second conceptualization of 'global' recognizes the multiple and plural ways of knowing and living which coexist with one another. It is this form of global which we argue is responsible, because it directs attention to the hegemonic processes of framing and circulation of meanings through which a certain global is produced at the expense of the local. Furthermore, as it is evident from much of the debate on climate change and the future unintended consequences of emerging technologies such as the impact on biodiversity, it is the local, specific and diverse that provides direction for further action and possibilities (Latour, 2018).

RI and RRI are two related but separate discourses that have emerged in parallel within contemporary science and public policy in the industrialized West in response to the failure of capitalism to recognize the limits of its own growth or to share the benefits of what growth has already occurred. Thus, what some would call global/universal really requires the imposition of Western social norms, values and worldviews, including definitions of the legitimate roles of democratic government, and an emphasis on material/Gross Domestic Product (GDP) growth. As we illustrated in Chapter 2, RRI is a discourse that has emerged almost exclusively from the European Commission, a policy artefact that advocates important agendas such as gender equality and open access, but in a quite incoherent way that reflects its origins as part of a flagship economic programme called Innovation Union. While these objectives are individually important, RRI has done little to challenge the status quo because responsibility for change is still positioned largely around existing policies and practices, leaving the universal–global model of innovation (in which the purpose of innovation is to increase productivity and boost economic growth) unchallenged, and if anything, re-enforced. In some cases, therefore, those who take action to preserve a particular aspect of local culture against the imposition of globalized monoculture (whether from North or South) are framed as being 'against progress', 'anti-global', 'anti-modernist' or, in short, Luddites. Yet, the Luddites were not in fact opposed to progress per se, they were opposed to the undermining of their traditional way of life as weavers, and to having machines control the pace of their work (Conniff, 2011).

If we are to take responsibility for our future in a world facing intertwined crises of sustainability, demographic change, inequality and insecurity, RRI, like the standard global model, offers little. RI, which has emerged from a largely academic tradition and uses a different approach to epistemology and a very different ontological worldview for innovation, appears to offer more possibility for a systemic change. It involves the adoption of processes or methods (activities of anticipation and reflexivity, greater inclusiveness of ideas and people and a mandate for responsive action among researchers and innovators) that can be applied to real innovation projects to foster responsibility. Nevertheless, this is also a discourse that is politically unresolved, one which is encountering significant challenges and indeed resistance as it runs into political agendas based largely on economic growth and productivity, and engrained institutional norms, cultures and organizational practices (as discussed in Chapter 7). We advocate for a far greater ambition, arguing for the need to reframe the very concept of 'innovation' (for example by including frames coming from the Global South) and to question the increasing number of institutions (in particular entrepreneurial universities) which are irreflexively coupled to it. To this end, scholars like Vasen (2017) and de Hoop and colleagues (2016) highlight significant limitations and argue that RI frameworks can still be prescriptive and emphasize principles that may not work in non-Western settings. This is not to say that RI and RRI do not have beneficial exportable qualities, but rather that they are likely to be received in multiple and variegated ways when applied to the context of the Global South. This in turn reveals to us, with a few notable exceptions, the banality of contemporary innovation, a project in which many are complicit, and many feel the need to change, but few feel empowered to do so.

What does it mean to be responsible globally?

As mentioned earlier, what is now global was once generally local to some place and time; it often requires a lot of power, persuasion and resources to turn the local into the global, the specific into the universal, and diversity into homogeneity. The processes by which this transformation happens often end up in excluding and destroying certain ways of knowing, innovating and being. Perhaps, as RI demands a 'commitment to care for the future through responsible stewardship of S&T in the present' (Stilgoe et al, 2013), a good starting point to understanding responsibility and RI in a global context is to pay attention to the hegemonic processes of framing and circulation of meanings through which a certain global is produced at the expense of the local. To be responsible globally, thus, means that there needs to be an active recognition that there are multiple futures and multiple time scales that are simultaneously unfolding and that sometimes these futures might be in tension and contestation with each other. A globalized economy and the soaring development of digital technologies might have created the illusion that we all have a common future on the planet, but its benefits and harms are definitely unevenly distributed in terms of power, wealth and other resources. Ulrich Beck (2002), in his highly acclaimed work on risk society, has clearly shown how the risks of unintended consequences of the future would have more negative impacts on the poverty-stricken, resource-deficient regions of the world (for example the impacts of the Chernobyl disaster in 1986 on the people and other species of Belarus, and the people still awaiting justice for the Bhopal Gas Tragedy in 1984 in India).

Similarly, if we look at the innovations in global value chains for goods, services and technologies, it is generally the people and resources of the politically unprivileged countries who are exploited to create surplus value for capitalist systems, very often in conditions which would not be tolerated in the West – the case of the Rana Plaza collapse in Bangladesh being an unforgettable example (Safi, 2018). At the same time, exploitation of the lower-income classes in the North is again on the rise. To be responsible globally, then, demands that it is not just possible but in fact essential that RI – and indeed RS – means different things in different contexts, so that specific needs and vulnerabilities in relation to local context, its present and its future are addressed. In particular, it requires that the vulnerable and dispossessed are given equal, if not privileged, status as stakeholders, decision makers and innovators.

The concern for context-specific engagement has led some scholars to suggest that in the context of the Global South, RI should engage with aspects of inequalities, informality and institutional capacity rather than future unintended consequences of emerging technologies (Vasen, 2017; Macnaghten and Chilvers, 2014). However, for the reasons mentioned earlier, we believe that in the present globalized scenario, where new technologies enter into people's world through uncharted terrains (for example, the sudden introduction of social media technologies in rural areas), these two questions are quite inseparable from each other in the context of the Global South. Often, the needs of the people in the Global South are conveniently defined in terms of measurements and indices that reassert the techno-economic paradigm. Thus, concepts used specifically for innovation in the Global South such as frugal, below-the-radar, bottom-of-the-pyramid and pro-poor end up representing people in terms of their economic capacity and relations, again favouring market and technological solutions, and those who benefit from such solutions. Such reasoning has resulted in numerous conflicts as people generally value other identities over the identity of 'consumer' (ecological and geographic connections, family relations, community membership and political citizenship), and solidarity and sharing over material growth (Beling et al, 2018; Kothari, 2014). The processes of critical reflection and inclusive deliberation as demanded in the RI framework also require close attention when discussed in the context of the Global South. Different communities and societies have their own mechanisms of reflection and deliberation that do not necessarily define engagement in limiting terms of expert-lay divides based on scientific literacy or access to modern S&T tools, thus privileging a specific set of actors over others.

We think that discussions of RS at a global level should be based on two basic pillars. Rather than pursuing economic growth per se, RS should help promote awareness that technological change (and thus innovation) should lead to a *global* social justice, the kind of 'global' that recognizes the multiple and plural ways of knowing and living. The second pillar, intimately connected to the first one, is that – as Boaventura de Sousa Santos (2015) argues – it is not possible to have a global social justice without a global cognitive justice. This refers to the creation of spaces (both within the conceptual space we have called the Fourth Quadrant and elsewhere) in which different sources of knowledge and ways of knowing can be articulated in what de Sousa Santos calls an 'ecology of knowledges'. This, in other words, means to care for the survival of different value systems and diverse ways of perceiving our role as humans on the planet without necessarily renouncing the achievements of modern S&T.

In Chapter 4 we suggested that 'governing with care' should be an essential feature of RS. In the global context we argue that this 'commitment to care' perspective, informed by feminist studies of techno-science, entails a recognition of multiple vulnerabilities and being attentive and caring for the most vulnerable and needy (Puig de la Bellacasa, 2015), making time for a slowed-down reasoning process and full exploration of alternatives before deciding whether to adopt a particular innovation, including the capacity to say no if it does not serve locally determined needs.

The lens of care also demands a reflection on the questions about who needs care, who has the capacity to care and who decides what or when care is needed. True caring also implies that the one who is cared for does not feel restricted, obliged, disrespected or powerless. A 'commitment to care' in the context of being responsible globally would mean caring for the most marginal and vulnerable communities, species, knowledge systems and ways of innovating. This also means that in order to be responsible globally, while thinking about our own future, it is important to constantly think about those whose future or present might get lost in the process of this realization. This can only be achieved if we focus on the relationalities between people, planet and things. For example, Puig de la Bellacasa (2015), in her study on soil rejuvenation strategies, shows how a care approach can highlight the relationalities through which different actors are tied to the soil and each other, and how caring for the pace of development of the most vulnerable (here, soil) is beneficial in the long run for humans, other beings and the entire planet.

An RS approach would allow the flourishing of multiple spaces for critical reflection on the purposes and usefulness of the techno-economic paradigm in a diverse world, supporting local concerns at a local level, rather than uncritically promoting the universality of one (formerly) local set of preferences. Given the pervasiveness of the hegemonic discourse that posits the universality of scientific rationality, we understand that this would require an enormous effort. At the moment, we struggle to find concrete and definite examples of how such an ecology of knowledges might look and operate in practice. Nevertheless, despite the hegemony of Western ways of innovating, alternative ways of framing post-growth innovation and technology that are remarkably based on responsibility and reflexivity can indeed be found in the South (see, for example, Escobar, 2011). These relate in many ways to the idea of RS because the frames change to support innovation around values and motivations that do not necessarily prioritize unsustainable economic growth. They draw on concepts such as autonomy, subsistence, conviviality

RESPONSIBILITY BEYOND GROWTH

and social justice. Although they have no aspiration to create a common front or to scale up (to use a phrasing very dear to classic development scholars), they testify to the social and political struggles that have arisen through the imposition of technical and scientific rationalities in the Global South and the myriad innovative ways people can respond.

Thus, the impetus to involve the public more deeply in the processes of research and innovation might look very different in the Global South. For example, a major focus of the People's Science Movement in India in the 1970s was to build technologies around local knowledge and resources in order to create democratic spaces where local communities could decide about the future (or the futures) they wanted for themselves (Pansera and Owen, 2018b). Leach and colleagues (2008) have also documented several cases in which technological development has been negotiated through reflexive and democratic processes that involve local communities, indigenous groups and, in general, a wider sector of civic society. More recently, the University of Cauca in Colombia has promoted within its Master of Interdisciplinary Development Studies degree the forum *Tramas y mingas para el Buen Vivir* [Conspiracy and Collaborations for Well-living]. These initiatives created a space in which indigenous and Afro-descendant intellectuals and activists, together with workers, women, environmentalists, peasants and urban activists, discussed the necessity to integrate different forms of knowledge, to rethink production and consumption, the design of new technologies, and education and democracy in Latin America.[5] Such encounters, attended by hundreds of participants, have been an amazing space of inter-epistemic conversation.

Other examples of innovations from the South that are worth mentioning come from a project called Smallholder Innovation for Resilience (SIFOR), which involved the work of 64 different indigenous communities in Kenya, India, China and Peru, developing what was labelled as biocultural innovations. These are defined as 'new ways of doing things (including new technologies) that emerge from interaction between components of biocultural heritage' (IIED, 2017). By blending traditional knowledge and science, the objective of the project was to examine the ways in which indigenous or traditional farming communities were developing their own innovations, in line with their cultural and spiritual values, framed under the Andean philosophy of *Buen Vivir* (in Quechua, *Sumak Kawsay*), which involves living in harmony between the environment, the community and their ancestral wisdom (Walsh, 2010). This resulted in the creation of a potato park in the sacred Valley of Peru, created and administered by five different communities and involving the exploration of different potato sources, which eventually resulted in the repatriation of 410 native potatoes, improved agroecological farming techniques, the revival of traditional seeds and knowledge exchange networks and potato rituals and ceremonies. The innovations identified by the project were the result of collaborations with other epistemic communities, for instance national and international universities, and institutes such as the International Potato Centre and more. The openness to share ideas and experiment in ways that fit within the indigenous cosmos, rather than a capitalist framework, shows a commitment to care informed by alternative ways of knowing and being. As such, this shows that – unlike considering indigenous knowledge as operating separately from scientific or other forms of knowledge – it is entirely possible to combine ways of knowing and working to find solutions to changes in the environment.

A similar attempt is the nationwide Alliance for Sustainable and Holistic Agriculture (ASHA) in India, which conducts agricultural fairs where farmers from all over India come together to share knowledge, expertise, seeds and equipment beyond the market economy. The initiative collectively aims for *Kisan Swaraj* (farmer self-rule),[6] making farmers gradually less dependent on agricultural multinational corporations. At the same time, they look for ecologically sensitive farming practices which can help with moving away from intensive and exploitative agriculture (ASHA, 2010).

These are only a few examples of the many initiatives that share some of the principles discussed elsewhere in this book. To go beyond that would require a full-fledged, long-term and much needed project on the possibilities of RS in the Global South, and a deep engagement with the field, far beyond what is possible in this volume. However, they do offer a glimpse of what is possible when the innovation process is truly shaped to engage with people's real needs, existing knowledges and cultural values.

We started this chapter by arguing that technology, far from being neutral, innocent, 'mere' tools, can be used as instrument of persuasion and domination. This intrinsic characteristic of technology has been used as a crucial part of national and colonial domination by certain powerful groups and countries, and continues by perpetuating the idea that poverty and underdevelopment can be overcome by technical innovation – usually framed within the ideological borders of market economics as defined by these same groups. We also argue that such innovation-led development projects pretend to be global and universal, laying claims to objectivity and universality in the way different human groups in different contexts frame their place in the world and envision their future, but this is not true. Given their origins in the North, RI and RRI are characterized by a similar process of ideological globalization that emphasizes the importance of being responsible within the context of Western elites' S&T paradigms. Here, RI and RRI emerged as a reflection on social, cultural and ethical aspects of innovation which re-emerged in the light of scientific and technological controversies such as fracking, nuclear weapons, genetic engineering and climate change, to mention but a few. Outside (and yes, sometimes even inside) the boundaries of the West, however, the notion of 'innovation' remains a contested term. This contested meaning of innovation makes it particularly difficult to articulate how technological development and, consequently, innovation can best be *responsible* according to Western formulations of RI.

We argue instead that technology in the Global South is more likely to be framed in a variety of different (sometimes radically different) forms that do not necessarily overlap with the idea of innovation as the engine of economic growth that is dominant in the North. Within this context, we advocate for a reformulation of responsibility that implies a commitment to care. RS, through its commitment to care about different knowledge systems, species, ways of knowing and innovating and, ultimately, different ways of living – inside, outside and against the market – offers such an approach. To advance in this direction, we advocate for RS as representing epistemological diversity in the framing of RI and RRI, to open up a space of debate and confrontation about a more appropriate, democratic and just way of framing technology in the Global South and among the dispossessed of the North. To be responsible globally in this context would mean appreciating, supporting and promoting these alternative ways of engagement and innovation. The focus should, however, lie not on mainstreaming certain alternatives, as they might reproduce the same social order and power structures (for example, mainstreaming organic farming has reproduced the techno-economic paradigm of scaling up, thus creating new vulnerabilities for marginal farmers). Rather, we stress maximizing the alternatives to achieve the full democratic potential of diversity.

Building on the discussion in Chapter 4, we suggest that a commitment to care is an ethico-political obligation to bring the perspectives of the marginalized and the invisible (which in turn can change in response to internal and external factors) to the fore. It is therefore a *continuous* commitment to be available and engaged, without exactly having a framework or a fixed answer. For this reason, we have explicitly avoided putting forward alternative structured frameworks for RI or RS, suggesting instead a set of aspects (configurations of change which stress living gently, restraint, ethics as central, and attention to scope and pace of decision-making). Having a framework or a standard format would in itself mean 'caring less', which is not a suitable proposition when we are talking about an uncertain future with unforeseen consequences, and the potential for loss of lives, livelihoods, species and irreversible damage to our planet. While RS in itself opens up possibilities to 'pause' or slow down, as discussed in Chapter 4, this slowness does not necessarily imply (or require) new frameworks to classify innovation or steps to follow. RS is not only about slowing down but also about enabling different knowledge systems and ways of living to coexist, to create a kind of harmonization in which each still retains its own distinctive character and tone. At the core of these ideas is the embrace of indigenous and local knowledges as valid and relevant. This involves not only thinking about RI and RRI in the way that has been framed by existing literature, but also using RS to challenge the discourse of development that subordinates indigenous knowledge to the demands of growth and progress. In essence, by highlighting alternative narratives of innovation 'of the people, by the people, for the people', we open RI/RS to understanding these experiences in their own right and allowing vastly diverse 'publics' to follow their own innovation trajectories and formulations of reflexivity and inclusive engagement.

7

Challenges Facing Willing Firms

Timothy Birabi

In Chapter 5, we mainly focussed on small businesses, 'not-for-profit' enterprises and social innovations primarily centred on integrating business activities with creating social value. In this chapter, the focus is much more on the corporation, in the broader institutional business sense of the word. Corporations are usually a large group of companies and may be involved with a very disparate host of activities, primarily seeking to achieve a central set of objectives, and having shares which are usually traded on public exchanges. By generalizing our discussion in this way, this chapter can treat the broader and often conflicting goals of creating value for shareholders versus creating more comprehensive societal (that is, stakeholder) value. This is perhaps the largest systemic obstacle to the particular configuration of social change represented by responsible stagnation (RS).

Corporate innovation in the current globalized market economy promotes a reward system with questionable social norms. It is a system where meta-national corporations expect to retain the positive returns accruing from their risk-driven investments. These corporations, however, also assume that the commons will resolve most of the negative consequences associated with these investments (as discussed in Chapter 3), for example problems such as waste and pollution, which are left for society to solve. As a result, some private companies accumulate wealth disproportionately compared to the negative public consequences of their actions, indeed often *because* the costs of those same actions have been passed on. The implications of such a system are vast because it propagates inequality while increasingly privatizing public wealth. It also fosters other undesirable economic outcomes, such as corporate tax avoidance, environmental degradation, wage deterioration and an increasing potential for the abuse of power as some corporations now control more wealth than many nation-states.

But what about the possibilities for actually trying to be a good, responsibly innovating business? This chapter explores some of the challenges companies who wish to adopt a more socially responsive business model face in free-market economies: the intangibility of capital, corporate accountability, and stockholder interests versus those of broader stakeholders. We also explore whether there might be further gains for businesses that act more responsibly very early on in their growth cycles or whether it is a much more critical strategy for prominent, mature companies that have relatively more at stake. In other words, can growth, innovation and responsibility coexist?

Corporate responsibility and innovation in the presence of intangible capital

As noted in Chapter 3, the free-market system does not always provide the best allocation of wealth, let alone responsibility. Regulation of the market is usually designed to force economic actors to internalize the full cost of their actions. It achieves this by disincentivizing unethical behaviour through increasing the compliance costs associated with engaging in societally undesirable corporate activities. These compliance costs have a direct impact on the reputational risk exposures and operational horizons of businesses, and this is why regulatory action can be socially beneficial. Unfortunately, much like an individual intending to dob in their partner in the Prisoner's Dilemma, when corporations gain (in spite of wrongdoing) by passing off the costs of their actions unto others it is considered 'just good business'. The political power dynamics are disproportionate, as corporations can and do lobby political systems to minimize their regulatory burdens to the barest minimum. Market capitalism exacerbates this phenomenon even further through its fundamental ethos for promoting 'small' governments. These are governments with limited policy choices, relegated to specific spheres, such as law and order and maintaining the rights of ownership, which in effect rewards corporations for their abdication of responsibility for addressing difficult issues.

Regulatory oversight is one of the primary mechanisms through which government departments can implement and enforce economy-wide corporate restraint, accountability and responsibility. However, modern growth-obsessed economies face a dilemma. Moves to reduce regulation to speed up innovation conflicts with the public's desire for governments to respond to the negative consequences of unconstrained corporate innovation. As noted already, the 'free' market is only free at the top, and only because the political economy is presently structured so that those with the least money and power bear most of the costs.

Increasingly, however, there is an awareness that this kind of innovation system is inherently *irresponsible* as the effects of climate change, inequality and resource depletion are becoming more apparent. The creation and legal empowerment of independent regulatory organizations, particularly in the EU, is one attempt at restoring some balance in the externalization of operating costs. Businesses are becoming increasingly aware of the market value of their social reputations and are adopting operational models which have various forms of 'corporate social responsibility' (CSR) as an integral add-on to their overall strategy (McWilliams and Siegel, 2001). Investors are also beginning to recognize that firms that act within a broader notion of social responsibility can gain a competitive advantage, and that their investments can indeed secure good returns in the long term, in spite of higher short-term adaptation costs.

All of this has created a more fertile field for responsible innovation (RI) discourses, particularly those aimed at 'a proper embedding of innovation in society' (von Schomberg, 2013)

– that is, successful sales figures. However, CSR programmes are highly variable. Some firms sincerely try to demonstrate responsibility to the communities in which they are embedded. For example, they might include post-activity restoration of a mining site into a public park as part of the plan for its exploitation, thus internalizing the associated social costs of their actions. Other firms operate in manners that appear to be little more than greenwashing; for example, advertising the absorption of waste production costs they are already required by law to absorb, or by making large donations to local schools while continuing to pollute. Real accountability is generally beyond the mandate of CSR programmes; indeed, they are often launched to avoid it. The add-on quality of CSR does not generally make these programmes an adequate stand-in for the kind of at-the-core ethics discussed in Chapter 4. It is possible to build social and environmental responsibility into the heart of a business strategy, as we shall discuss later in this chapter. However, we will first discuss the restraints.

Two main developments in private enterprise could help explain why it is increasingly challenging for businesses to innovate responsibly in the presence of modern capital. One is the formation of limited liability business structures, first enacted into law in 1977 in Wyoming, US, which eventually affected how business entities would operate the world over. What this legal precedence offered was protections for stockholders, corporate investors, owners, boards and managers from being held directly liable for any financial liabilities arising from the business. As a result, it created a business environment that legally separated stockholders from the full consequences of their investments and allowed business owners and investors to pass the liabilities of irresponsible business practices on to the 'corporate entity'. These business structures did not, however, limit their ability to reap substantial returns when things went well.

The Wyoming precedent reinforced the ethos that a firm's sole social responsibility is to maximize profit for its shareholders in any way legally possible (Friedman, 2007). However, this strong position has increasingly come under scrutiny. Short-term objectives can often yield zero-sum outcomes, that is, where equal losses offset any benefits; meanwhile, equity gains for stockholders too often come at the expense of other stakeholders, particularly employees. The alternative viewpoint is for businesses (and stockholders) to take a more long-term view of profit-making, one which seeks to optimize a lifetime profit curve naturally conditioned on realizing gains to all stakeholders involved with their enterprise. In this manner, they can maximize the firm's social and economic licence to operate over an infinite time horizon.

The second development is that intangible capital (non-physical attributes such as human relationships, knowledge, branding, intellectual property and so on) significantly affects the ephemerality of the corporate entity. Their consequences on organizational behaviour have become most apparent and established as economies, cultures and polities become ever more interconnected through globalization. Businesses must adapt by creating more competitive (that is, cheaper) ways of operating to provide their products and services. Many companies can now do this without the restrictions of being physically present in the locales where they accumulate profit, aided by the commercialization opportunities of the internet. This means that the modern marketplace is overall becoming less physical, and demand fulfilment no longer requires businesses to have local sales outlets. These fulfilments can now be almost completely virtual, accessed via online platforms that simultaneously provision multiple geographies, with only the storage and transport of goods taking place in the physical world.

In their book, *Capitalism Without Capital*, Jonathan Haskel and Stian Westlake (2018) write about the four main properties of modern intangible capital which together are gradually transforming capitalist economies into 'intangible economies': scalable, sunk, synergetic and spillover. These pose difficult and often unremarked challenges for integrating RI at the corporate level, and so are worthy of a closer look before we continue.

Scalable capital is designed to be used repeatedly, in several places simultaneously, with little or no reinvestment required, which reduces the liability of irresponsible businesses. At the moment, it is increasingly difficult to tie the bulk of the activities of big corporations to a single geographical location. Essentially, businesses can bypass the operational standard implemented and enforced in country A by moving to country B, where operational costs and social demands for corporate accountability are lower. This allows behemoth corporations to operate globally while largely avoiding taxation, thus retaining more of their profits to disperse to shareholders, but also incentivizing social irresponsibility.

To a large extent, this explains the 'race to the bottom' phenomenon that local authorities in most countries currently face. Ideally, local authorities should enforce fair tax regimes on profitable companies to strengthen their tax revenue positions and support income distribution within society. However, we find that they instead design competitively favourable tax regimes to attract these kinds of businesses to their locales in the hope of obtaining other benefits, such as jobs and local spending by employees. Unfortunately, the resulting socio-economic result has been that such a system propagates inequality along with all its accompanying societal challenges, with corporations and their leaders paying a significantly lower percentage of tax compared to relatively smaller local companies and typical members of the public.

The *sunken* property of intangible capital reduces its convertibility when things go wrong or when these businesses fail. When companies have the bulk of their wealth in the form of physical assets, it often acts as some insurance to mitigate risks to investors. If and when such businesses fail, their assets could be repossessed, liquidated and used to compensate debt-holders, stockholders, and other vested stakeholders – such as employees. Tangible property also makes union activities and strike actions quite practical, as these can block access to the place of employment and thus force management to the bargaining table. It becomes much more of a challenge to operate similarly when the bulk of a business's assets are ephemeral or intangible. It is not difficult to see how this kind of system incentivizes risk-taking beyond what the market can price into the real value of innovation. These days, we find many businesses overvalued for this very reason. The real value of these types of companies often only gets revealed following significant reputational damage. It is also near-impossible for governments to obtain damage repair costs on behalf of society and its comprising individuals from the failing business. There is usually nothing left of the company to liquidate, as most of the initial investments, sunk into misvalued ephemeral assets, are now non-transferrable and worthless. The costs of such corporate failures often accrue to the non-irresponsible stakeholders in the form of pensions lost to former employees, and external costs are often left to governments and local authorities to address using limited taxpayers' money.

The last two properties of intangible capital highlighted in Haskel and Westlake's (2018) work, *synergies* and *spillovers*, incentivize modern businesses to prioritize value capture over value creation. Synergies implies that intangible capital captures more value when adopted in combination with other intangible capital. Assets rich in synergic properties are even more valuable if deployed in ways that harness the spillover opportunities from other related innovations. Corporations do this so that they will be able to retain or capture as much value from existing innovations while attempting to prevent the outflows of positive externalities from their own. This strategy explains why internet platform monopolies have been able to harness gains from public goods such as the World Wide Web. At the same time, they have also been able to stockpile large portfolios of patented web solutions, algorithms, products and services built on top of these public goods. The synergic and spillover properties of capital incentivize corporations to dedicate more of their resources to incremental innovation instead of radical innovations, which create truly new ways of doing things. Incremental innovations, on the other hand, benefit from past radical innovations and are preferable for businesses who simply want to retain as many benefits as possible for themselves from these existing ideas.

However, the story is not all gloom. An increasing number of corporate innovators in platform economies[1] are now starting to seek out opportunities to create positive externalities to society. This strategy focuses on creating spillover value to the general public by attempting to counterbalance some of the adverse effects detailed earlier. As publics become more conscious of issues like climate change and unethical work practices (and direct their purchasing accordingly), there is a renewed drive to seek out new ways of doing business to demonstrate that corporate enterprise can be a force for both profit-making and generating social good. The role of digital technology in providing solutions to critical social challenges is therefore increasing, particularly where there is still profit to be made, for example in delivering educational programmes at a distance. Thus, predominant modern corporate strategies often involve seeking out opportunities to harness all four properties of the intangibility of capital – scalable, sunken, spillover, synergy. However, even companies which may be seeking to demonstrate altruistic behaviour through beneficial spillovers will find that they are limited by the need to deliver shareholder value if publicly traded.

The shareholder–stakeholder dichotomy

The question of to whom businesses are responsible or accountable brings several ethical issues to the fore. It is not clear how a business's accountability to its stockholders affects its responsibility to the environment and its collaborating stakeholders (such as other players in the market and employees). Businesses' supposed responsibilities to their collaborating stakeholders may well conflict with their accountability to their investing stockholders. In his frequently reprinted *New York Times* article, the US economist Milton Friedman (2007, p 178) concluded that 'there is one and only one social responsibility of business: to use its resources and engage in activities designed to increase its profits so long as it stays within the rules of the game...' Friedman's purpose was to direct 'responsibility' solely towards accountability to investing stockholders, calling any other discussion of social responsibility in business 'pure and unadulterated socialism'. While it is tempting to poke at the morality of Friedman's position, it is nonetheless crucial to note that it is compliant with the minimum legal requirements of stakeholder responsibility, that is, that businesses ought to pay a minimum wage to their employee-stakeholders, pollute only within the legally permitted maximum with regards to the environment-stakeholder and uphold human rights and other legal obligations to their society-based stakeholders. Democratic governments can, of course, amend the rules of the game to ensure that existing institutional dynamics do not sideline the interests of the other stakeholders, but corporations can also undermine this, as noted earlier, by influencing the political process in their favour.

However, Friedman did accept that both goals could converge if *investors* desired formalized social goals (emphasis added). In that case, management would have no choice but to deliver these socially desirable goals for their stockholders (with resulting benefit to other stakeholders as a spillover effect). What the stockholder versus stakeholder angle brings to the narrative is that responsibility and accountability are, but do not have to be, two distinct issues for businesses. The Friedman school of thought argues that CSR (in the real sense of internalizing costs) undermines the accountability of organizational management to their investing shareholders, positing that pursuing social responsibility rather than stockholder returns can lead to the collapse of free-enterprise as we know it. Friedman feared that profit-making businesses might thus dwindle in favour of societally accountable companies that generate less financial wealth overall. Whether that would really mean less overall *prosperity* (given that socially responsible companies might be more likely to pay their workers well, so they would have more disposable income to spend) is very much the kind of question that discussions of RS begs.

Additionally, Grayson and Hodges (2017) suggest that businesses often consider corporate responsibility as an afterthought. As businesses grow, the potential reputational costs of running an enterprise that ignores the bigger picture of responsibility and accountability often forces them to consider bolting on CSR programmes. There are several reasons why corporate growth may naturally precede their responsibility and duty to the public. First, it could merely be that bigger businesses are better able to afford to make these social investments. Their favourable financial position frees up resources to engage in socially impacting activities. As a result, we often find that there is a link between enterprise size and the capacity for creating social value beyond shareholder profits.

Secondly, large businesses with mainly intangible capital are vulnerable to potential reputational changes, having a more complex network of systemic risk exposures and being more susceptible to share value fluctuations from reputational dynamics than a company which is not publicly traded. Although large companies often benefit from their well-connected global networks of operations, this can sometimes work against them. As these global operational networks get even denser, they also must adopt increasingly convoluted risk frameworks to maintain their competitive edge. As a result, they are not always able to maintain a uniform operational corporate model and identity across ensuing geographies with different laws, regulatory requirements and cultures. Eventually, such intricately connected businesses are more vulnerable to accusations of irresponsibility somewhere along their supply chains.

Corporate responsibility and accountability may thus gradually become a necessary condition to elicit and retain trust from consumers as firms establish themselves as dominant players in the market. Consumers, as members of society, expect more prominent, established enterprises to start giving back to the communities that have supported their growth thus far. There is an increasing risk of damage to a business's reputation with every missed opportunity to fulfil this unwritten social contract of reciprocity. It may cost the business more to behave more responsibly than legally required, but this may be paid back by goodwill from their customer base and a more established social licence to operate. However, CSR programmes must be perceived as sincere and meaningful in order for this reciprocity to work.

One of the increasingly popular ways a corporation can distinguish its brands is by engaging with real social challenges in order to increase its intangible capital as a business interested in more than just profit-making. In Chapter 5 we discussed social innovation, a model which certainly does allow a business to put a social goal first, but these kinds of businesses are generally not-for-profit or third sector organizations. However, the desire of entrepreneurs and investing stockholders to make profits does not always have to be de facto antithetical to that of creating social value.

Responsible stagnation in business: the Benefit Corporation

The ubiquity of the Friedman model created a legal position in which shareholders could actually sue the company if it attempted to be more responsible – for instance, if using above-standard production methods in order to reduce environmental impacts negatively affected shareholder returns. To counter this, Wall Street private equity investor Andrew Kassoy and two of his friends, Jay Coen Gilbert and Bart Houlahan, started the non-profit B Lab in 2006 (Honeyman, 2014). B Lab created an alternative benefit corporation legal structure and also issues the B Corp certification. Businesses using the legal structure can go one step further and become certified B Corps based on a rigorous assessment of their practices, demonstrating that they are committed to meeting a high standard of transparency, accountability and sustainability, and to developing their businesses with the purpose of creating a 'material positive impact on society and the environment ... to consider the impact of their decisions not only on shareholders but also on workers, the community, and the environment' (B Lab, 2020). Unlike traditional shareholders, investors in B Corps cannot sue if ethical decision-making reduces investment returns. Instead, they can sue the company for not living up to its primary philanthropic obligations.

The B Corp movement has shown that it is possible to pursue and attain both stockholder and stakeholder value simultaneously, and there are now over 3,000 companies registered around the world.[2] While most B Corps are small, privately owned businesses, there are also large, publicly traded multinational corporations like Natura, well-known brands such as Ben & Jerry's Ice Cream and Etsy, even lawyers, banks and financial services companies. The B Lab position suggests that the primary duty of corporations to their stockholders is not necessarily in conflict with their social responsibility to their collaborating stakeholders. It is possible to view both goals as strategic complements rather than strategic substitutes. A business could, as a matter of competitive strategy, differentiate its brand to all prospective investors, employees and consumers as one with a longer-term goal to cultivate and harness responsible forms of innovation, whether or not it is called RI. We can already see a steady rise of environment and social governance (ESG) reporting and ESG-investing. There is also a rise in consumers using their purchasing patterns to demonstrate their selective loyalty to more responsible brands.

Prominent corporations have a lot to gain by distinguishing themselves as ethical, therefore, even without B Corp certification, and are increasingly open to responsible branding as a viable corporate strategy as the public's taste for this increases. This also tends to communicate to investors looking for ethical alternatives that a company is committed to a sustainable long-term growth strategy (Sethi, 2005). There is increasing evidence in the literature that ethical investment indices now perform as well as market indices, often without the same amount of volatility or associated risks (Manos and Drori, 2016, p 20).

In other words, both positions – Friedman and B Corp – are valid, but indicate two alternative pathways for RI. In one, the corporation can pursue a narrowly defined stockholder profit mission, constrained by the law, yet still seeking to aim innovation at social needs, because that is what the market presently demands. Alternatively, businesses can pursue a more broadly balanced mandate where they still seek to maximize profit, but within the ecological constraints of the planet and the highest social standards. As a form of for-market RS, we would argue that at this particular point in time the B Corp perspective may indeed put the corporation in a more advantageous spot over the longer term, and is more likely to shape their innovation activities in ways which cohere with restraint, living gently, slower decision-making and care. Because B Corps tend to be much closer to their customers, this also opens possibilities for innovating in partnership with communities, even across the globe (as part of the B Corp certification process is a whole value-chain approach.)

A classic example of this movement is the outdoor equipment company Patagonia, which engages in extensive R&D with scientific and industrial partners for what might be called innovation for stagnation, such as developing a plant-based substitute for the petroleum-based neoprene commonly used in wetsuits.[3] Patagonia focuses heavily on reducing its production footprint (water consumed and/or carbon produced) and improving the quality, sustainability and recyclability of its products, most of which are now made from reclaimed textiles. They have also worked to reduce their supplying farmers' exposure to the toxic pesticides used for producing cotton by switching to organic alternatives. At the time, this was a substantially risky innovation, and there was concern that because organic options have a much higher production cost this could potentially put the company out of business. By choosing a modest price increase coupled with reduction in both the variety of products for sale and predicted profit margins, the company proved such transitions were possible and Patagonia became a primary enabler of the organic cotton movement. However, the company is probably most famous for taking out ads in major US newspapers on Black Friday in 2011 asking people *not* to buy their products.[4] The ads detailed the precise environmental footprint of one of their most popular jackets, and suggested that people should not buy things they do not need. Instead, they have made it possible to recycle and repair Patagonia goods for free.

Patagonia's specific clientele tends to be environmentally conscious, and so it has a great deal of leeway for this kind of RS which might not exist in other industries. But partly as a result of their actions, competition in the outdoor equipment industry is now not just about pricing and quality, but also about demonstrating who has the most sustainable and ethical manufacturing and labour practices along the whole of their supply chain. Patagonia's business model conforms very closely to the kind of a-growth approach to innovation we have been discussing throughout this book, and in fact is largely a result of creditors calling in their loans during the 1991 recession, a disaster which nearly bankrupted the company and has made its founder growth-wary ever since (Chouinard, 2013). As a form of RS in for-market innovation, Patagonia and other B Corps demonstrate that it is possible to place social and environmental concerns first, and still grow – the company was valued at over $700m by 2017.[5] Additionally, it self-taxes 1 per cent of sales to be donated to environmental charities and allows employees time off to do research or join campaigns.

Can economic growth, innovation and public accountability coexist?

Mainstream economic literature posits that technological progress through corporate innovation is a vital source of growth in the macroeconomy (Barro, 1996; Solow, 1956; Swan, 1956). Within this neoclassical economic growth framework, the place for restraint in the form of corporate responsibility or accountability is almost non-existent. As a result of the ever-increasing consequences of unfettered growth and its accompanying technological innovations, the need for effective regulatory action is on the rise, but in most countries is often not met. This means that business sectors exhibiting the most innovative activities, such as finance, pharmaceuticals and the life sciences, are coming under increasing public demand for more cautious progress and constraints on price-induced growth. These are sectors with the potential to significantly affect human lives. These are also sectors that have enormous funding pools, and from which venture capitalists and corporate stockholders expect significantly high investment returns. As the financial crisis showed, when growth is the sole focus of innovative behaviour, it can result in very undesirable, even irresponsible innovative investments, and regulatory activities may in fact support the risky practices they are meant to curb. As discussed in Chapter 3, this is one of the reasons why markets, in and of themselves, cannot deliver the kind of socially beneficial innovation RI demands.

We further suggest that this kind of growth, although faster on the surface, is suboptimal and shallow, first because it leads to an unequal redistribution of economic and political power and second, because it is increasingly unsustainable from both an ecological and reputational level as customers' tastes progressively move towards choices based not only on costs and benefits to themselves, but on promoting social justice and preserving the habitability of the planet.

Secondly, this kind of growth has clearly resulted in an uneven form of human development. Growth that is about thriving economically, but is indifferent to social and environmental costs, is only partial progress. As they search for real prosperity instead of having a narrow focus on economic growth at any cost, B Corps show there is room for a more encompassing idea of social development embracing every aspect of society, even within the for-profit business sector. To this we contribute the idea of RS as a philosophical shift in the way we view innovation, and its contribution to improving the quality of all life on the planet.

PART IV

Responsibility in the Fourth Quadrant

The responsible innovation matrix presented in the introduction contrasts 'responsibility' with 'irresponsibility', and 'innovation' with 'stagnation'. While the quadrant representing RI has been much discussed, we began with the idea that the quadrant of responsible stagnation (RS) had gone largely unexplored, and we wanted to know what that might mean and what kinds of activities it might describe.

As it turned out, this Fourth Quadrant was actually full of innovation, in a broader and wider sense than might be expected by the term 'RS'. But thinking of RI as part of a matrix, of responsibility as having impact on *both* innovation and stagnation, and stagnation as something that could be beneficial in certain circumstances, allowed us to decouple our thinking from growth and markets, and focus instead on what we really need innovation to do.

We take the idea of RS seriously, as a means to try to grasp the complexity of the political economy of science, technology and innovation (STI), both as policy and as process, as we take the Fourth Quadrant seriously as a space for considering innovation in business models as well as in non-market-oriented processes, goods and services which may have strong societal benefit but do not necessarily contribute to Gross Domestic Product (GDP). In our concluding section, we argue that RS offers its own innovative contribution to the growing global discussion about RI, recalibrated around responsibility as its focal point, rather than getting more things to the market.

127

Thus, it allows us to more carefully examine the conundrum of diminishing returns and increased environmental and social hazards associated with attempts to merely increase activities that can be measured by GDP.

As there is no one-size 'how-to' which will fit all, our aim with this last section is not a practical set of recommendations on how to innovate for RS. Instead, we offer a compass for the expansion of RI policies and discourses, pointing towards opportunities for creative thinking about the meaning of innovation and its relationship to prosperity and progress.

8

Conclusion: The Scope of Responsible Stagnation

Stevienna de Saille, Fabien Medvecky
and Michiel van Oudheusden

We started this book reflecting on Joseph Stiglitz's unfulfilled prediction of 2009 – that following the global economic crisis, the current dominant economic system would need to enact profound change. So far, this has not been the case. There is nothing new in pointing this out, nor that devotion to free-market, laissez-faire capitalism is inseparable from our inability to address increasingly disruptive health, environmental and social concerns. However, there is at last a rumble from across the globe (even from institutions such as the World Economic Forum!) that suggests a growing agreement that our present socio-economic systems are 'no longer fit for purpose' (Schwab, 2017). Indeed, the COVID-19 pandemic has laid bare the harm that has been done to public health and social support systems over the last ten years in search of GDP growth. It may be argued that this has exacerbated the pandemic's impact, leaving even the richest countries desperately short of equipment and medical personnel, and forcing governments to implement vast welfare programmes to support the millions of workers finding themselves suddenly unemployed, policies which would have been unthinkable just weeks before.

But pointing out the shortcomings of the present system is only half the battle. The other half is to offer viable alternatives, to imagine a better economic and social system and to find steps to reach it from where we are, based on innovation in the broadest sense of that word. We understand that what we have discussed here so far may not represent the kind of truly radical change that many people – including many of us – would like to see. But it is also possible that what appears now to be a rather small change in the way we think about innovation is, in fact, the beginning of a much bigger re-imaging of 'the system' than we could realize any other way.

Of course, we don't just want to innovate; we want to innovate responsibly. Echoing David Guston (2015), who could be against that? Innovating responsibly obviously requires we take both 'responsibility' and 'innovation' seriously, as we should. But, as we have argued, it also requires a careful look at responsibility and stagnation as well, and how these terms can change in specific contexts. It requires we think through what all these terms really mean, and what kind of work they do, how they can push our thinking outside the box, but also hold it rigidly within the system we know.

As we argued at the start, stagnation in innovation in the broad sense is not possible. We will always want to know what happens if we put this and that together, if we do the same thing a different way, if we try something else to meet our needs. We will always want others to know we came up with something better, and if we have, it's likely they will want it too. But the current policy discourse around innovation is embedded in a specific economic framework, a market-driven form of capitalism which seeks a specific form of growth which is classically measured by a specific indicator, Gross Domestic Product (GDP).

To illustrate our point, we offer this example: if someone buys £3 worth of ingredients and contributes the equivalent of £7 worth of labour at home to make lasagna, they only contribute £3 to GDP, as 'household production' is not included in this measure. But if they sell the lasagna to someone else pre-made, that would instead add £10 to GDP as labour costs now count.

Similarly, if a charity receives a £100 donation to feed the homeless, they could feed 33 people on £3 worth of ingredients each (thanks to our volunteers' labour), rather than just ten if the meals are purchased complete. While the same £100 is added to GDP either way, its qualitative, real-world value is now actually £330 and we have grown our ability to feed the homeless by 23.

Acknowledging that GDP responds only to for-market innovation (not to mention only one particular conception of growth) opens up the Fourth Quadrant of the innovation matrix, responsible stagnation (RS). This is a conceptual space in which we can gather to trade ideas, projects, models – and yes, innovations – which can go beyond the epistemic limitations of our present system to consider more creative solutions to the problems that we face. Some of our ideas are as old as Adam Smith and John Stuart Mill, and some stem from relatively new fields, such as ecological economics. However, they all suggest roughly the same thing: that past a certain point, growth is neither feasible nor necessarily beneficial. For example, Daly's (1991) vision of a steady-state economy (SSE), like other challenges to the growth-centred paradigm, is motivated by two core observations: first, that the current GPD growth trajectory is not sustainable given the limited environmental stock available, and second, that continuing economic growth beyond that already achieved in developed countries does not necessarily lead to a bettering of the lives of the individuals in these countries. GDP, he argues, is not a useful measure of economic health, precisely *because* it 'conflates qualitative improvement (development) with quantitative increase (growth)' (Daly, 2007, p 15).

The usefulness of GDP is central to the difference between orthodox and heterodox economic visions of growth. The former holds that we should strive for sustained economic growth as measured by GDP, underpinned by an assumption that development occurs in tandem, and technological progress is key to both. The latter holds that we need other measures, since growth, development and progress are not so neatly linked or mapped onto GDP, and that stagnation – if viewed, as Daly does, as the economy coming to an overall balance between production and consumption – may not be such a terrible thing.

This leads us to question how we might innovate responsibly, rather than simply trying to accelerate growth.

Techno-science and responsible stagnation

There is an understandable reluctance to interference with technologies which represent a significant investment in R&D, particularly where these have developed strong industrial sectors and lobbying groups, even when there is clear evidence that problems are arising 'downstream' (that is, once the technology begins to be taken up in numbers large enough to see the effects). However, without consideration also being given to the question of establishing when, and by what mechanisms, it might be determined that a trajectory of innovation should be changed, slowed or even stopped, there may be a further erosion of public trust in both science and in the political establishment's ability (or willingness) to safeguard society's collective interests and respond to legitimate concerns about the pace and trajectory of technological change.

In such instances, responsibility may be better enacted through a deliberate slowing down or even pause in the pace of innovation while negative impacts are assessed and necessary changes (for instance, new regulations) are developed. A corollary to this might include working to restore or maintain balance in a disrupted sector which is deemed beneficial for reasons other than economic growth (for example, health and education), or to minimize social disruption when a technological sector needs to be phased out (as in the case of fossil fuels). This brings us to a second definition of RS: what novel ideas, arrangements, rules, funding streams and so on, as well as new technologies, goods and services would be required if we were to aim innovation not at growth for the sake of growth, but at reducing and reusing what we already have, at conserving irreplaceable resources and public wealth?

This is the key conundrum for innovation within current economic frameworks: while responsible innovation (RI) is meant to direct innovation towards cooperative solutions to globalized problems such as climate change, the economic paradigm in which it is embedded calls for increasing economic transactions, even if this implies continued extraction of diminishing resources or a disregard for mass unemployment. Market-based innovation, therefore, occurs in a context in which it is unlikely all, or even most, members of society will share its benefits, let alone have the political capital to engage with its direction – a lacuna which the RI literature also tends to neglect (van Oudheusden, 2014). We suggest that a deeper exploration of arguments and models stemming from other economic schools, particularly from ecological and steady-state economics, might help provide insight into the kind of macroeconomic paradigm which RI would require in order to fulfil its call for innovation which can 'respond to the needs and ambitions of society' (EC, 2012) and provide real solutions – some of which might not be technical at all – to the complex problems we face.

Throughout this book, we have argued that these kinds of questions, and the kind of innovation that happens within what we have called the Fourth Quadrant, can point us towards what we need – new ideas, models, systems, technologies and social relations to help us mitigate the damage we have already incurred in the search for GDP-measured growth. Solutions to our pressing problems, we argue, need to be developed not by bracketing or ignoring social and environmental costs, but instead by bracketing their contribution to GDP. We have called this 'RS' partly because it embraces the idea that finding ways to slow down, to reduce or maybe even stop doing or making some things *is* sometimes the most responsible form of innovation. But we also want to be responsible by doing this carefully, in ways that consider and try to mitigate the systemic effects of change – be that deliberate or driven by catastrophic events – particularly on those with the least economic and political power.

RS also acknowledges the fact that post-industrial economies have for some time been in a state of secular stagnation that may well be permanent. In these economies, we argue for seeking new pathways towards maintaining a prosperous way of life, rather than only searching for ways to increase GDP-measured growth. We advocate an a-growth approach to innovation because we do not think contribution to GDP (or lack thereof) should be the most important criterion for determining the benefits and harms of new things, and because the dominant growth paradigm excludes as valuable the many kinds of innovation and economic activity which cannot be captured by GDP, but which are nevertheless always taking place. However, we also advocate paying very careful attention to how these ideas get applied to countries which are *not* past their productivity peak. Citizens of such countries may indeed still gain from the kind of growth GDP is meant to measure in terms of being able to meet their basic needs, but they may also have their own ideas about what constitutes beneficial economic activity and RI.

We do not think that responsible stagnation is going to be simple. The complexity of our present situation is staggering and we do not want to pretend for a moment that it is not. Fourth Quadrant thinking is also about trying to take into account what else happens if we do enact the kinds of stagnation that we would like to see, particularly in an economic system in which even having a guaranteed full-time job is often not enough to make ends meet. Justified criticism has been aimed at CEOs who are paid over a thousand times more than their employees, and to behemoth corporations which generate billions in profit, pay little tax and yet still refuse to pay their workers a truly living wage. But caught up in this cycle of secular stagnation are also numerous small to medium firms desperately struggling to survive. Many of these enterprises are, in fact, trying to make and do things we might think of as RS – seeking to use less, to do things better, to work with business models that value the planet, their workers and society at large. Even more are caught up in the global production chains that begin in factories, fields and homes across the world and end with a delivery to our door. Fourth Quadrant thinking must also seek to avoid the kind of outcome where the costs of mitigation are shifted onto those who can least afford it, or where not buying certain products means that across the world we may cause a whole village to starve as their jobs disappear. RS asks, and will continue asking, *how can we balance a necessary reduction in material consumption with a world in which we can all afford to live and prosper?*

RS argues that job precarity and low wages are not, as so often claimed, a result of stagnation, but rather the product of decisions made in the service of particular ideas embedded in the GDP-growth paradigm about raising productivity through driving down labour costs. As with outsourcing, this model long predates the crisis of 2008. However, the economic system cannot sustainably produce increasing levels of GDP by reducing labour costs, as workers who cannot pay their bills have no spare cash to spend, thus negating the beneficial purpose (and often the actuality) of any productivity gains, while at the same time increasing demands made on a diminishing tax base. Changes to the way corporations are taxed, which are necessary and welcome, could solve many problems in terms of funding social services like health, education and pensions, but it will not solve the fundamental problems of energy provision, and managing waste and pollution. More money for research and market-based innovation will not necessarily help historically exploited nations to create health, education and welfare systems which can address their own societal aspirations if they remain the low-wage producers of what is consumed elsewhere.

As discussed in Chapters 3 and 7, however, the problem goes beyond the ubiquity of GDP as the key measure against which so many other things – national debt, investment, trade deficits, government spending, and so on – are assessed. There is also the uncritical equation of increases to GDP with increases in individual wellbeing, despite the fact that a rise in consumption of many goods and services, such as those required for rebuilding after environmental disasters or increased sales of alcohol, pharmaceuticals and counselling services to desperately stressed people, indicate quite the opposite is taking place. As also previously noted, growth is rarely evenly distributed, and GDP does not distinguish between mansions purchased by billionaires and the building of affordable homes for the poor. But growth is also generally linked to a beggar-thy-neighbour culture in which resolving the Prisoners' Dilemma by harnessing the rewards of self-interest is socially valued over cooperating on the expectation that both will then prosper.

This presents other difficulties for supporting innovation which can truly address the kinds of problems that governments, social enterprises, charities and non-profits do not have the resources to solve, and in which the market often has little interest – or in some cases, may actively resist. There are increasing numbers of businesses, both large and small, which are trying to develop innovations which address these areas by, for example, using carbon waste gases as feedstock for genetically altered bacteria which then produce combustible fuel, or seeking biodegradable substitutes for common plastics. However, these research programmes are often dependent upon limited public funds which must be topped up by private investment, and investors often expect to see returns much faster than they actually tend to occur when something is truly novel. Often this shifts innovation not towards the most useful new thing, but towards the one which can be achieved the fastest, or can be sold for the most profit. Corporations with shareholders have even more constraints, as these have been shaped almost exclusively to externalize costs such as pollution as much as legally possible in order to produce the highest returns, which in turn attracts investors solely looking for wealth creation. While there is increasing evidence that investors themselves are beginning to shift towards responsibility as a criterion, seeking opportunities to support the creation of beneficial technologies or businesses with ethical goals, such efforts still need considerable structural transformation at the economic and political level in order to exert a change effect on the system overall.

Revisiting the components of responsible stagnation

Because of all of this, we have argued that we need to look at innovation from an a-growth perspective, and see what possibilities this opens up. In this final section, we'd like to return to where we began: with five ideas which can be used as a way to make sense of these questions, and of the possibility of responsible stagnation. Think of these as spotlights that draw attention to areas which are especially contributive when thinking about prosperity instead of growth: a **pool of great ideas** supporting **a particular configuration of change**, where **ethics matters** as we aim towards **restraint** and **living gently** in the world.

Rather than a criticism of RI discourses and frameworks, we see RS as a constructive project to imagine and develop alternative and complementary courses of responsibly innovative action to support what we need, without always seeking more.

Its utility will be dependent on how all stakeholders (policy makers, industry players, scientists and technologists, civil society groups, citizens) engage with the ideas, values and considerations that sustain it, such as responsibility, care and agnosticism to growth. As this book has shown, RS is already happening in many places and in many ways. Within this **pool of great ideas**, there are already some hints and indications as to where these might lead and what kind of configuration of change RS gestures towards. The answers, we feel, are already in the system, it is largely a matter of the political willingness to find ways to support them.

RS is **a particular configuration of change** because it unfolds with RI and in response to the dominant innovation-for-growth paradigm. It provides possible alternatives to these frameworks by questioning the assumptions that underpin demands for growth, and by pointing out how a broader conception of innovation enhances the ultimate goal of making and doing things better. RS instils in us a capacity for critical self-reflection on the norms, assumptions and aims that guide present-day political and economic agendas, thereby opening new opportunities and venues for genuinely responsible approaches to innovation. Pointing to the many existing alternatives enables us to explore our present modes of thinking and doing and wonder what else could be different, and how we might develop and support models and values based on qualitative, rather than quantitative growth. We might then ask: how does this or that innovation change or challenge our politics? How does it interact with our economic system? Does it really improve things, and for whom? Would less actually be not more, but better?

Integrating social and ethical concerns into the innovation process is one way of shaping not just the solutions, but the scope of questions which can be asked. However, this also requires that the innovation system has the capacity to respond. Participation in the governance of science and technology (S&T) could go beyond the somewhat limited vision of RI, which focusses largely on emerging technologies and formal innovation systems. As we have noted throughout, a configuration of change that looks beyond the market is likely to find people participating in all kinds of novel means of knowledge generation and economic exchange which are locally relevant and contribute to their prosperity – a state of flourishing, happiness and wellbeing, irrespective of monetary wealth.

This kind of innovation is inherently linked to ethics. By claiming that **ethics matters**, we aim to highlight that ethical consideration is not to be seen as an add-on to the innovation, but as an integral part of it, guiding the trajectory of innovation away from winner-take-all and more towards the collective gains of cooperation. In fact, we want to make a stronger case. We want to claim that ethical considerations, in particular an ethics of care, should be the starting point of our innovating, guiding where we focus our efforts and how we proceed. We also make the case that ethical considerations stretch beyond just the innovation itself, that we need to consider the ethical implications of the systems and structures within which we innovate, and how our innovating reinforces and perpetuates the systems and norms within which we live. Some we may well want to reinforce, while others we need to question, challenge and reconsider. By stating that ethics matters, we draw attention to the normative underpinnings of innovations and invite the aspirational. We highlight questions that are not always evident in the nitty-gritty of innovation: why these innovations? Why not others? Whose needs do they serve? Who or what is excluded, controlled, or (re/de)valued, and why? How could innovation be otherwise?

In line with the idea that stagnation can be a responsible choice, we would like to re-valorize the idea of **restraint**. Much innovation presently serves pointless accumulation, as innovation-for-growth by default encourages over-consumption as a way of life. Planned obsolescence and other means of encouraging people to buy things they neither want nor need may be good for GDP, but it subtracts profoundly from prosperity both now and in the future as materials are consumed and waste produced for no real beneficial purpose. We see this particularly playing out in the North/South inequalities discussed in Chapter 6, and in the devaluation and transfer of public goods into private hands. But innovating with restraint also means revamping some of our production and consumption models, particularly those which encourage solutions in search of a problem, or innovating just to sell more. RS allows us to consider instead if innovation would increase real benefit, if the need for it exists, and how improving production might create disruption all along the value chain, taking into account jobs lost as well as jobs created, and the fact that these rarely affect the same groups of people. Restraint invites new questions, such as 'do we really need this innovation now?'

Personal prosperity, in the form of happiness and wellbeing, is not significantly affected when we cease to consume what we do not really need, and concentrate instead on making what we do need better by improving the longevity of goods or designing products to be repaired, rather than replaced. This supports the idea of **living gently** and having care for the costs externalized to both human and non-human alike, of being aware of the ecological impact of a proposed innovation, as well as innovating purposely to mitigate existing planetary damage. It points us towards increasing innovation which helps us by replacing non-renewable resources, making useful things out of what we presently throw away, or considering what products and services might need regulation on a global, rather than national, scale.

Responsibility beyond growth

These illustrations open onto another important value inherent in both RS and RI. Responsibility requires oversight, which in turn requires public engagement with science, technology and innovation (STI). We need to value the relationships we hold, with the planet and with each other, and we need to hold them with care, which means we also need a greater breadth of voices talking about a greater breadth of topics. Complex problems such as climate change, nuclear waste management, or novel viruses emerging from formerly undeveloped areas create irreversible consequences for peoples and ecosystems across the world. It is thus not surprising that ever more societal actors (civil society organizations, interest groups, citizens) are demanding a right to participate in how such issues are framed and handled. In some instances, citizens now even produce their own scientific data and research tools, set their own research agendas, and produce reliable scientific knowledge (Irwin, 1995). This is because traditional representative democracy, industrial science, and the 'free market' may fall short of grasping the complexity of the issues at play; they may discount any limits to growth, or fail to represent the wide diversity of stakes or to develop a comprehensive 'evidence base' on which to formulate and promote policy. Orthodox market and innovation policies contribute to, and exacerbate, the costs these problems bring with them for communities and environments. They 'lock in' to socially disruptive and environmentally unsustainable choices even when knowledge challenging these choices is readily available to decision makers, who are prone to reject this evidence because they fear the effects of short-term loss of profit or slower growth, particularly in a crisis period. Greater public engagement with our various innovation systems (beyond merely encouraging more people to become entrepreneurs) is one way to guide these systems towards more sustainable, more cooperative, longer-term values.

But the changes we propose with engagement, social innovation and more responsible firms will not just materialize on their own; they must be embedded, enabled and incentivized within the larger economic-political structure of innovation. The state has an essential role to play in these processes, both as a financial provider of research and innovation funding, and as having the capacity to offer incentives towards RS when this is needed. It should not retreat into the background (as has been the prevailing trend in developed countries); rather, the state needs to do its work differently, by strengthening the capacity to explore a variety of approaches to innovation, and by accepting that it has a responsibility to promote prosperity for all its citizens, not just those it considers economically productive.

To sum up, the Fourth Quadrant of the innovation matrix provides a space in which important underlying assumptions can be made visible and questioned, opening possibilities for innovation directed at achieving social, ecological and economic equilibrium and for reducing input rather than always seeking to produce more. Sometimes it may be the case that innovation outside or even against the market, is the better, most responsible course of action. RS invites us to keep in mind that innovation is something we value and seek for its capacity to make things better, not merely to generate growth.

Thinking in terms of RS may help to find (and define) a more optimal balance for new sectors, and incorporate better ways to measure and value environmental and social costs and benefits, including the distribution of negative impact such as environmental depletion and job losses, to offset the rhetoric of jobs created and GDP achieved. RI then becomes not just a matter of upstream public engagement to successfully embed an innovation in the market, but a way of using anticipation and reflexivity to consider the most socially and environmentally responsible pathways to reach a specific goal, and then developing the best solutions for achieving it.

It would be a mistake, however, to view RS as an alternative to RI, to claim that we can engage in either RI or RS, but not both. Responsibility forms two quadrants in the matrix which are intimately connected, and we should traverse these freely. We do not demand the reader agree with each and every observation we have raised herein, but we ask for these to be received in the spirit of critical self-inquiry which RI encourages, by reflecting on the norms, assumptions and aims that inform our present innovation systems. This, in turn, may lead to the development of alternative conceptions of innovation, which can then be considered, weighed and assessed against one other, given the specific problem and context we need to address. In order to truly progress, rather than destroying ourselves and our planet, we need to have the space to ask a broader range of questions, to consider what is really needed, to *care*. We need, quite frankly, to innovate 'innovation'.

Notes

Chapter 1

[1] The value of all goods and services produced within a national boundary within a given period.

[2] A good discussion of attempts to solve this problem with other metrics can be found in Fleurbaey (2009).

[3] The precursor to GDP for measuring the health of a national economy, GNP reflects the value of goods and services produced by a country's residents, regardless of where produced. Thus, a Japanese-owned car factory in Detroit contributes to the GDP of the US, not Japan, but is included in Japan's GNP.

[4] While the field is too diverse to discuss in depth here, the *Journal of Ecological Economics* provides a good start for the reader who would like to delve deeper.

[5] See www.freecycle.org/about/missionstatement.

[6] An account of this evolution can be found in de Saille, 2015. For a broader look at the formative discussions around RI, see Owen et al, 2013a.

[7] de Saille and Medvecky, 2016, adapted from Guston, 2015, p 2, Figure 1.

[8] An excellent discussion of the co-evolution of science, markets and money can be found in Yuval Noah Harari's *Sapiens* (2014). We note that Harari emphasizes the necessity of cooperation for human progress, rather than competition.

[9] A conclusion echoed even by the World Economic Forum at Davos (see Cann, 2018).

Chapter 2

[1] A US-based organization from the 1970s, which is presently undergoing a resurgence: https://scienceforthepeople.org/.

[2] Good discussions of these issues can be found in the *Journal of Responsible Innovation*.

Chapter 3

[1] There are a number of accessible treatments of the financial crash for the reader who would like more detail, among them Lanchester (2010) and Stiglitz (2009).

[2] See Groves and Ledyard (1977) for a theoretical treatment.

Chapter 5

[1] According to Schumpeter, innovation is the driver of a long-term process of structural change of the economy, fuelled by profit-seeking entrepreneurs and technological change (Schumpeter, 1942).

[2] http://one.laptop.org

[3] It should be noted, however, that the original purpose of the M-Pesa application was to enable collection of micro-finance loans (Morawczynski 2009).

[4] https://www.jaipurfoot.org/

[5] www.barefootcollege.org

[6] www.goodgym.org

[7] https://extranet.who.int/kobe_centre/en/project-details/community-based-social-innovations

[8] www.issmich.at

[9] www.fairphone.com/en/blog/?ref=homecta

[10] https://wfto.com/about-us/history-wfto/history-fair-trade

[11] https://timebanks.org/about

[12] https://tsimanifesto.org/manifesto

Chapter 6

[1] For good discussions of these claims, see also Feenberg, 1999; Pinch and Bijker, 1984; Winner, 1993.

[2] We use RRI here to denote the EU framework and RI to denote the broader scope of discussion arising in various parts of the world.

[3] See Pansera and Owen (2018b) for a detailed analysis of this shift.

[4] See various policy documents such as *Innovation and Inclusive Development* (Paunov, 2013) and *The Growth Report: Strategies for Sustained Growth and Inclusive Development* (World Bank, 2008).

[5] https://tramasymingasparaelbuenvivir.wordpress.com/

[6] www.kisanswaraj.in/about/

Chapter 7

[1] These are online businesses which derive income from facilitating connections between buyer and seller, such as Ebay, Uber or Airbnb.

[2] https://bcorporation.net

[3] www.patagonia.com/yulex.html

4   www.patagonia.com/blog/2011/11/dont-buy-this-jacket-black-friday-and-the-new-york-times/

5   www.businessoffashion.com/articles/news-analysis/how-patagonia-transformed-the-circular-economy

References

Akemu, O., Whiteman, G. and Kennedy, S. (2016) 'Social enterprise emergence from social movement activism: the Fairphone case', *Journal of Management Studies*, 53(5): 846–77.

Amanatidou, E., Gritzas, G., Kavoulakos, K.I. (2015) 'Time banks, co-production and foresight: intertwined towards an alternative future', *Foresight*, 17(4): 308–31.

Amanatidou, E., Gagliardi, D. and Cox, D. (2018) 'Social Engagement: Towards a Typology of Social Innovation', *MIOIR/MBS Working Paper Series – Working Paper, Vol. 82*. Available from: www.research.manchester.ac.uk/portal/files/66664922/MIOIRWP82_SI_AmanatidouetalMar2018_1_.pdf [Accessed January 2020].

Andreyeva, T., Blumenthal, D.M., Schwartz, M.B., Long, M.W. and Brownell, K.D. (2008) 'Availability and prices of foods across stores and neighborhoods: the case of New Haven, Connecticut', *Health Affairs*, 27(5): 1381–8.

Arnold, D. (2013) 'Nehruvian Science and Postcolonial India', *Isis*, 104(2), pp. 360–70.

Arnstein, S.R. (1969) 'A ladder of citizen participation', *Journal of the American Institute of Planners*, 35(4): 216–24.

Asante, K., Owen, R. and Williamson, G. (2014) 'Governance of new product development and perceptions of responsible innovation in the financial sector: insights from an ethnographic case study', *Journal of Responsible Innovation*, 1(1): 9–30.

ASHA (2010) 'About', *Alliance for Sustainable and Holistic Agriculture*. Available from: www.kisanswaraj.in/about/ [Accessed August 2019].

B Lab (2020) 'How Do I Create General Public Benefit?' *Benefitcorp.net*. Available from: https://benefitcorp.net/how-do-i-create-general-public-benefit [Accessed January 2020].

Barro, R.J. (1996) *Determinants of Economic Growth: A Cross-Country Empirical Study*, Cambridge, MA: MIT Press.

Bator, F.M. (1958) 'The anatomy of market failure', *The Quarterly Journal of Economics*, 72(3): 351–79.

Beck, U. (2002) 'The Cosmopolitan Society and its Enemies', *Theory, Culture & Society*, 19(1–2), pp. 17–44.

Becker, G.S. (1968) 'Crime and punishment: an economic approach', *The Journal of Political Economy*, 76(2): 169–217.

Beling, A.E., Vanhulst, J., Demaria, F., Rabi, V., Carballo, A.E. and Pelenc, J. (2018) 'Discursive synergies for a "great transformation" towards sustainability: pragmatic contributions to a necessary dialogue between human development, degrowth, and Buen Vivir', *Ecological Economics*, 144: 304–13.

Berg, P. (2008) 'Meetings that changed the world: Asilomar 1975: DNA modification secured', *Nature*, 455 (7211): 290–1.

Blauwhof, F.B. (2012) 'Overcoming accumulation: is a capitalist steady-state economy possible?', *Ecological Economics*, 84: 254–61.

Blok, V. and Lemmens, P. (2015) 'The emerging concept of responsible innovation. Three reasons why it is questionable and calls for a radical transformation of the concept of innovation', in B. Koops, I. Oosterlaken, H. Romijn, T. Swierstra and J. van den Hoven (eds) *Responsible Innovation 2*, Zurich: Springer, pp 19–35.

Boulianne, M., Fraisse L. and Ortiz, H. (2003) 'Économie solidaire et mondialisation', *Revue Du Mauss Paris*, 21: 47–54.

Boyle, D. (2005) 'Sustainability and Social Assets: The Potential of Time Banks and Co-Production'. Available from: https://timebanks.org/wp-content/uploads/2011/08/GrassrootsFoundation.pdf [Accessed December 2019].

Bryan, D., Martin, R., Montgomerie, J. and Williams, K. (2012) 'An important failure: knowledge limits and the financial crisis', *Economy and Society*, 41(3), 299–315.

Calvário, R. and Kallis, G. (2016) 'Alternative food economies and transformative politics in times of crisis: insights from the Basque Country and Greece', *Antipode*, 49(3): 597–616.

Cann, O. (2018) 'Focus on GDP Fuelling Inequality and Short-Termism', *World Economic Forum*. Available from: www.weforum.org/press/2018/01/focus-on-gdp-fuelling-inequality-and-short-termism [Accessed December 2019].

Cave, T. and Rowell, A. (2014) *A Quiet Word: Lobbying, Crony Capitalism and Broken Politics in Britain*, London: The Bodley Head.

Chouinard, Y. (2013) 'Prosperity With Less: What Would A Responsible Economy Look Like?', *The Guardian*, 4 October. Available from: https://www.theguardian.com/sustainable-business/patagonia-founder-responsible-economy-with-less [Accessed December 2019].

Clifton, J. (2019) 'Is it Time to Retire Global Unemployment?', *Gallup Blog*, 10 December, https://news.gallup.com/opinion/gallup/268922/time-retire-unemployment.aspx [Accessed 6 January 2020].

Collingridge, D. (1981) *The Social Control of Technology*, London: Palgrave Macmillan.

Conniff, R. (2011) 'What the Luddites Really Fought Against', *Smithsonian Magazine*. Available from: www.smithsonianmag.com/history/what-the-luddites-really-fought-against-264412 [Accessed January 2020].

Daly, H. (1991) *Steady-State Economics* (2nd edn) [1977], Washington, DC: Island Press.

Daly, H. (2007) *Ecological Economics and Sustainable Development, Selected Essays*, Cheltenham: Edward Elgar.

de Hoop, E., Auke P. and Romijn, H. (2016) 'Limits to responsible innovation', *Journal of Responsible Innovation*, 3(2): 110–34.

de Saille, S. (2015) 'Innovating innovation policy: the emergence of "responsible research and innovation"', *Journal of Responsible Innovation*, 2(2): 152–68.

de Saille, S. and Medvecky, F. (2016) 'Innovation for a steady state: a case for responsible stagnation', *Economy and Society*, 45(1): 1–23.

de Sousa Santos, B. (2015) *Epistemologies of the South: Justice Against Epistemicide*, New York: Routledge.

Dietz, R. and O'Neill, D. (2013) *Enough is Enough: Building a Sustainable Economy in a World of Finite Resources*, London: Routledge.

Doz, Y.L. and Kosonen, M. (2010) 'Embedding strategic agility: a leadership agenda for accelerating business model renewal', *Long Range Planning*, 43(2–3): 370–82.

Drucker, P.F. (1957) *Landmarks of Tomorrow: A Report on the New Post-Modern World*, New York: Harper & Row.

EC [European Commission] (2010a) *Europe 2020 Flagship Initiative: Innovation Union* [SEC(2010) 1161]. Available from: https://op.europa.eu/s/nDqr [Accessed June 2019].

EC (2010b) *Knowledge for Growth: Prospects for Science, Technology and Innovation*. Available from: https://op.europa.eu/s/nXHM [Accessed November 2019].

EC (2012) *Responsible Research and Innovation: Europe's Ability to Respond to Societal Challenges*. Available from: https://op.europa.eu/s/nDqz [Accessed December 2019].

EC (2013) *Options for Strengthening Responsible Research and Innovation*. Available from: https://op.europa.eu/s/nv8O [Accessed November 2019].

EC (2016) *Open Innovation, Open Science, Open to the World – A Vision for Europe*. Available from: https://op.europa.eu/s/nXta [Accessed November 2019].

EC (2019a) 'Science with and for Society', *Horizon* 2020. Available from: https://ec.europa.eu/programmes/horizon2020/en/h2020-section/science-and-society [Accessed December 2019].

EC (2019b) 'Social Innovation'. Available from: https://ec.europa.eu/growth/industry/innovation/policy/social_en [Accessed August 2019].

Edwards-Schachter, M. and Wallace, M.L. (2017) '"Shaken, but not stirred": sixty years of defining social innovation', *Technological Forecasting and Social Change*, 119(C): 64–79.

Escobar, A. (2011) 'Sustainability: design for the pluriverse', *Development*, 54(2): 137–40.

Escobar, A. (2012) *Encountering Development: The Making and Unmaking of the Third World* (2nd edn), Princeton: Princeton University Press.

Etzioni, A. (2004) *The Common Good*, Malden, MA: Polity Press.

Feenberg, A. (1999) *Questioning Technology*, Oxon: Routledge.

Felt, U., Wynne, B., Callon, M., Gonçalves, E., Jasanoff, S., Jepsen, M., Joly, P-B. et al (2007) *Taking European Knowledge Society Seriously*. Available from: https://op.europa.eu/s/nDqv [Accessed November 2019].

Fioramonti, L. (2017) 'Gross domestic problem: how the politics of GDP shaped society and the world', in I. Borowy and M. Schmelzer (eds) *History of the Future of Economic Growth*, Oxon: Routledge, pp 91–109.

Fisher, E. and Rip, A. (2013) 'Responsible innovation: multi-level dynamics and soft intervention practices', in R. Owen, J. Bessant and M. Heintz (eds) *Responsible Innovation: Managing the Responsible Emergence of Science and Innovation in Society*, Chichester: John Wiley & Sons, pp 165–83.

Fleurbaey, M. (2009) 'Beyond GDP: the quest for a measure of social welfare', *Journal of Economic Literature*, 47(4): 1029–75.

Flyvbjerg, B. (1998) 'Habermas and Foucault: thinkers for civil society?', *British Journal of Sociology*, 49(2): 210–33.

Foucault, M. (1972) *Histoire de la folie à l'âge classique: Folie et déraison*, Paris: Gallimard.

Freeman, C. (1987) *Technology, Policy, and Economic Performance: Lessons From Japan*, New York: Frances Printer.

Fressoli, M., Arond, El., Abrol, D., Smith, A., Ely, A. and Dias, R. (2014) 'When grassroots innovation movements encounter mainstream institutions: implications for models of inclusive innovation', *Innovation and Development*, 4(2): 277–92.

Friedman, B.M. (2006) 'The moral consequences of economic growth', *Society*, 43(2): 15–22.

Friedman, M. (1962) *Capitalism and Freedom*, Chicago: University of Chicago Press.

Friedman, M. (2007) 'The social responsibility of business is to increase its profits', in W.C. Zimmerli, M. Holzinger and K. Richter (eds) *Corporate Ethics and Corporate Governance*, Berlin: Springer, pp 173–8.

Friedman, M. and Friedman, R. (1980) *Free to Choose: A Personal Statement*, New York: Harcourt Brace Jovanovich.

Funtowicz, S.O. and Ravetz, J.R. (1993) 'Science for the post-normal age', *Futures*, 25(7): 735–55.

Gabriel, M. (2016) 'Policy for Social Innovation: Five Ways Policy Can Support Social Innovation', *Social Innovation Community* blog, 3 October. Available from: www.siceurope. eu/policy-portal/policy-social-innovation-five-ways-policy-can-support-social-innovation [Accessed August 2019].

Gibson-Graham, JK. (2010) 'Forging post-development partnerships', in A. Pike, A. Rodriguez-Pose and J. Tomaney (eds) *Handbook of Local and Regional Development*, London: Routledge, pp 226–36.

Gilbert, N. (2013) 'A hard look at GM crops', *Nature*, 497(7447): 24–6.

Gilligan, C. (1995) 'Moral orientation and moral development [1987]', in V. Held (ed) *Justice and Care*, London: Routledge, pp 31–46.

Gismondi, M. (1997) 'Sociology and environmental impact assessment', *Canadian Journal of Sociology*, 22(4): 457–79.

Grayson, D. and Hodges, A. (2017) *Corporate Social Opportunity!: Seven Steps to Make Corporate Social Responsibility Work for Your Business*, Abingdon: Routledge.

Grimm, R., Fox, C., Baines, S. and Albertson, K. (2013) 'Social innovation, an answer to contemporary societal challenges? Locating the concept in theory and practice', *Innovation: The European Journal of Social Science Research*, 26(4): 436–55.

Grinbaum, A. and Groves, C. (2013) 'What is "responsible" about responsible innovation? Understanding the ethical issues', in R. Owen, J. Bessant and M. Heintz (eds) *Responsible Innovation: Managing the Responsible Emergence of Science and Innovation in Society*, Chichester: John Wiley & Sons, pp 119–42.

Groves, T. and Ledyard, J. (1977) 'Optimal allocation of public goods: a solution to the "free rider" problem', *Econometrica*, 45(4): 783–809.

Guston, D.H. (2015) 'Responsible innovation: who could be against that?' *Journal of Responsible Innovation*, 2(1): 1–4.

Haidt, J. (2001) 'The emotional dog and its rational tail: a social intuitionist approach to moral judgment', *Psychological Review*, 108(4): 814–34.

Harari, Y.N. (2014) *Sapiens*, London: Random House.

Hardin, G. (1968) 'The tragedy of the commons', *Science*, 162(3859): 1243–8.

Harding, S. (2011) 'Beyond postcolonial theory' in S. Harding (ed) *The Postcolonial Science and Technology Studies Reader*, Durham and London: Duke University Press.

Haskel, J. and Westlake, S. (2018) *Capitalism Without Capital: The Rise of the Intangible Economy*, Princeton: Princeton University Press.

Haucke, F.V. (2018) 'Smartphone-enabled social change: evidence from the Fairphone case?' *Journal of Cleaner Production*, 197: 1719–30.

Haxeltine A., Kemp, R., Dumitru, A., Avelino, F., Pel B. and Wittmayer, J. (2015) *TRANSIT WP3 deliverable D3.2 – 'A First Prototype of TSI Theory'*. Available from: www.transitsocialinnovation.eu/resource-hub/transit-wp3-delverable-d32-a-first-prototype-of-tsi-theory [Accessed December 2019].

Held, V. (2006) *The Ethics of Care: Personal, Political, and Global*, Oxford: Oxford University Press.

Holloway, K.J. (2015) 'Normalizing complaint: scientists and the challenge of commercialization', *Science, Technology, & Human Values*, 40(5): 744–65.

Honeyman, R. (2014) 'A look at the history of the B Corp movement', *Triple Pundit* blog, 19 August. Available from: www.triplepundit.com/story/2014/look-history-b-corp-movement/41536 [Accessed January 2020].

Hubbard, G., Garnett, A. and Lewis, P. (2012) *Essentials of Economics*, Melbourne, VIC: Pearson Higher Education AU.

IIED (2017) 'Smallholder Innovation for Resilience (SIFOR)', *International Institute for Environmental Development – Biocultural Heritage*. Available from: https://biocultural.iied.org/smallholder-innovation-resilience-sifor [Accessed August 2019].

Irwin, A. (1995) *Citizen Science: A Study of People, Expertise and Sustainable Development*, Oxon: Routledge.

Jackson, T. (2009) *Prosperity Without Growth: Economics for a Finite Planet*, London: Routledge.

Jackson, T. (2018) *The Post-Growth Challenge – Secular Stagnation, Inequality and the Limits to Growth*, Centre for the Understanding of Sustainable Prosperity (CUSP) Working Paper No 12, Guildford: University of Surrey. Available from: www.cusp.ac.uk/publications [Accessed December 2019].

Jackson, T. and McBride, N. (2005) *Measuring Progress?: A Review of 'Adjusted' Measures of Economic Welfare in Europe*, Centre for Environmental Strategy Working Paper 11/05, Guildford: University of Surrey. Available from: http://www.surrey.ac.uk/ces/files/pdf/1105-WP-Measuring-Progress-final.pdf [Accessed December 2019].

Jasanoff, S. and Kim, S-H. (2009) 'Containing the atom: sociotechnical imaginaries and nuclear power in the United States and South Korea', *Minerva*, 47(2): 119–46.

Kahn, A.E. (1966) 'The tyranny of small decisions: market failures, imperfections, and the limits of economics', *Kyklos*, 19(1): 23–47.

Kahneman, D. (2011) *Thinking, Fast and Slow*, New York: Allen Lane.

Kerr, A., Hill, R.L. and Till, C. (2018) 'The limits of responsible innovation: exploring care, vulnerability and precision medicine', *Technology in Society*, 52: 24–31.

Keynes, J.M. (1963) 'Economic possibilities for our grandchildren (1930)' in *Essays in Persuasion*, New York: W.W. Norton & Co., pp 358–73.

Klein, J.-L., Fontan, J.-M., Harrisson, D. and Levesque, B. (2013) 'The Quebec Model: a social innovation system founded on cooperation and consensus building' in F. Moulaert, D. MacCallum, A. Mehmood and A. Hamdouch (eds) *The International Handbook on Social Innovation*, Cheltenham: Edward Elgar, pp 371–83.

Kolk, A., Rivera-Santos, M. and Rufin, C. (2013) 'Reviewing a decade of research on the "base/bottom of the pyramid" (BOP) concept', *Business & Society*, 20(10): 2–40.

Kothari, A. (2014) 'India 2100: towards radical ecological democracy', *Futures*, 56: 62–72.

Kubiszewski, I., Costanza, R., Franco, C., Lawn, P., Talberth, J., Jackson, T. and Aylmer, C. (2013) 'Beyond GDP: measuring and achieving global genuine progress', *Ecological Economics*, 93: 57–68.

Kuznets, S. (1962) 'How to judge quality', *The New Republic*, 147(16): 29–32.

Lanchester, J. (2010) *IOU: Why Everyone Owes Everyone and No One Can Pay*, New York: Simon and Schuster.

Latour, B. (2018) *Down to Earth*, Cambridge, MA: Polity Press.

Lawn, P.A. (2003) 'A theoretical foundation to support the index of sustainable economic welfare (ISEW), genuine progress indicator (GPI), and other related indexes', *Ecological Economics*, 44(1): 105–18.

Leach, M., Sumner, A. and Waldman, L. (2008) 'Discourses, dynamics and disquiet: multiple knowledges in science, society and development', *Journal of International Development*, 20(6): 727–38.

Legge Jr, J.S. and Durant, R.F. (2010) 'Public opinion, risk assessment, and biotechnology: lessons from attitudes toward genetically modified foods in the European Union', *Review of Policy Research*, 27(1): 59-76.

Levidow, L. (1998) 'Democratizing technology or technologizing democracy? Regulating agricultural biotechnology in Europe', *Technology in Society*, 20(2): 211–26.

Lövbrand, E., Pielke Jr, R. and Beck, S. (2011) 'A democracy paradox in studies of science and technology', *Science, Technology, & Human Values*, 36(4): 474–96.

Macnaghten, P. and Chilvers, J. (2014) 'The future of science governance: publics, policies, practices', *Environment and Planning C: Government and Policy*, 32(3): 530–48.

Macnaghten, P., Kearnes, M. and Wynne, B. (2005) 'Nanotechnology, governance, and public deliberation: what role for the social sciences?', *Science Communication*, 27(2): 1–24.

Macnaghten, P., Davies, S.R. and Kearnes, M. (2015) 'Understanding public responses to emerging technologies: a narrative approach', *Journal of Environmental Policy & Planning*, 21(5): 1–19.

Mancini, M.S., Galli, A., Niccolucci, V., Lin, D., Bastianoni, S., Wackernagel, M. and Marchettini, N. (2016) 'Ecological footprint: refining the carbon footprint calculation', *Ecological Indicators*, 61(2): 390–403.

Manos, R. and Drori, I. (eds) (2016) *Corporate Responsibility: Social Action, Institutions And Governance*, Berlin: Springer.

Marcuse, H. (1966) *One Dimensional Man: Studies in Ideology of Advanced Industrial Society*, Boston: Beacon Press.

Martin, B. R. (2012) 'The evolution of science policy and innovation studies', *Research Policy*, 41(7), pp. 1219–39.

Massey, D. (2005) 'The spatial construction of youth cultures', in Skelton, T. and Valentine, G. (eds) *Cool Places: Geographies of Youth Culture*, pp 120–29, London: Routledge.

McWilliams, A. and Siegel, D. (2001) 'Corporate social responsibility: a theory of the firm perspective', *Academy of Management Review*, 26(1): 117–27.

Merton, R.K. (1968) 'The Matthew effect in science', *Science*, 159(3810): 56–63.

Mill, J.S. (1909) *Principles of Political Economy with Some of their Applications to Social Philosophy* [1848] (7th edn), London: Longmans, Green and Co.

Morawczynski, O. (2009) 'Exploring the usage and impact of "transformational" mobile financial services: the case of M-PESA in Kenya', *Journal of Eastern African Studies*, 3(3): 509–25.

Moulaert, F., Martinelli, F., Swyngedouw, E. and Gonzalez, S. (2005) 'Towards alternative model(s) of local innovation', *Urban Studies*, 42(11): 1969–90.

Mumford, M.D. (2002) 'Social innovation: ten cases from Benjamin Franklin', *Creativity Research Journal*, 14(2): 253–66.

Murray, R., Caulier-Grice,J. and Mulgan, G. (2010) *The Open Book of Social Innovation*. Available from: https://www. nesta.org.uk/report/the-open-book-of-social-innovation/ [Accessed February 2020].

Nietzsche, F.W. (1908) *Human, All Too Human: A Book for Free Spirits*, Chicago: Charles H. Kerr & Company.

NRC [National Research Council] (2008) *Innovative Flanders: Innovation Policies for the 21st Century: Report of a Symposium*, Washington, DC: The National Academies Press.

OECD (2015) *The Innovation Imperative: Contributing to Productivity, Growth and Well-Being*, Paris: OECD Publishing.

Ostrom, E. (1990) *Governing the Commons: The Evolution of Institutions for Collective Action*, New York: Cambridge University Press.

Owen, R., Macnaghten, P. and Stilgoe, J. (2012) 'Responsible research and innovation: from science in society to science for society, with society', *Science and Public Policy*, 39: 751–60.

Owen, R., Bessant, J. and Heintz, M. (eds) (2013a) *Responsible Innovation: Managing the Responsible Emergence of Science and Innovation in Society*, Chichester: John Wiley & Sons.

Owen, R., Stilgoe, J., Macnaghten, P., Gorman, M., Fisher, E. and Guston, D. (2013b) 'A framework for responsible innovation', in R. Owen, J. Bessant and M. Heintz (eds) *Responsible Innovation: Managing the Responsible Emergence of Science and Innovation in Society*, Chichester: John Wiley & Sons, pp 27–50.

Pansera, M. (2018) 'Frugal or fair? The unfulfilled promises of frugal innovation', *Technology Innovation Management Review*, 8(4): 6–14.

Pansera, M. and Martinez, F. (2017) 'Innovation for development and poverty reduction: an integrative literature review', *Journal of Management Development*, 36(1), pp. 2–13.

Pansera, M. and Owen, R. (2018a) 'Framing inclusive innovation within the discourse of development: insights from case studies in India', *Research Policy*, 47(1): 23–34.

Pansera, M. and Owen, R. (2018b) *Innovation and Development: The Politics at the Bottom of the Pyramid*, London: ISTE-Wiley.

Pansera, M. and Owen, R. (2018c) 'Innovation for de-growth: a case study of counter-hegemonic practices from Kerala, India', *Journal of Cleaner Production*, 197(2): 1872–83.

Paunov, C. (2013) *Innovation and Inclusive Development: A Discussion of the Main Policy Issues*, Paris: OECD Publishing.

Peredo, A. (2012) 'The BOP discourse as capitalist hegemony', *Academy of Management Proceedings*, 2012(1): 1–1.

Pinch, T.J. and Bijker, W.E. (1984) 'The social construction of facts and artefacts: or how the sociology of science and the sociology of technology might benefit each other', *Social Studies of Science*, 14(3): 399–441.

Polyani, K. (2001) *The Great Transformation* [1944], New York: Farrar & Rinehart.

Prakash, G. (1999) *Another Reason: Science and the Imagination of Modern India*, Princeton: Princeton University Press.

Puig de la Bellacasa, M. (2015) 'Making time for soil: technoscientific futurity and the pace of care', *Social Studies of Science*, 45(5): 691–716.

Quiggin, J. (2010) *Zombie Economics: How Dead Ideas Still Walk Among Us*, Princeton: Princeton University Press.

Raworth, K. (2017) *Doughnut Economics: Seven Ways to Think Like a 21st-Century Economist*, White River Junction, VT: Chelsea Green Publishing.

Rist, G. (2007) 'Development as a buzzword', *Development in Practice*, 17(4–5): 485–91.

Rogers, K. (2008) *Participatory Democracy, Science and Technology. An Exploration in the Philosophy of Science*, Basingstoke: Palgrave.

Royal Society (2019) 'New and emerging technologies', *Royal Society*. Available from: https://royalsociety.org/topics-policy/new-emerging-technology/topic/ [Accessed November 2019].

RRI Tools Consortium (2016) 'A Practical Guide to Responsible Research and Innovation: Key Lessons from RRI Tools', *RRI Tools Consortium*. Available from: www.rri-tools.eu [Accessed November 2019].

Safi, M. (2018) 'Rana Plaza, Five Years On: Safety of Workers Hangs in Balance in Bangladesh', *The Guardian*, [online] 24 April. Available from: www.theguardian.com/global-development/2018/apr/24/bangladeshi-police-target-garment-workers-union-rana-plaza-five-years-on [Accessed 12 August 2019].

Saltelli, A., Benessia, A., Funtowicz, S. et al (2016) *The Rightful Place of Science: Science on the Verge,* Tempe, AZ: Consortium for Science, Policy & Outcomes.

Samuelson, P.A. (1954) 'The pure theory of public expenditure', *The Review of Economics and Statistics*, 36(4): 387–9.

Samuelson, P.A. (1956) 'Social indifference curves', *The Quarterly Journal of Economics*, 70(1): 1–22.

Scheidel, W. (2018) *The Great Leveler: Violence and the History of Inequality from the Stone Age to the Twenty-First Century*, Princeton, NJ: Princeton University Press.

Schumpeter, J.A. (1942) *Capitalism, Socialism and Democracy*, London: Routledge.

Schwab, K. (2017) 'We Need a New Narrative for Globalization', *World Economic Forum*. Available from: www.weforum. org/agenda/2017/03/klaus-schwab-new-narrative-for-globalization [Accessed December 2019].

Seabright, P. (2004) *The Company of Strangers: A Natural History of Economic Life*, Princeton, NJ: Princeton University Press.

Sethi, S.P. (2005) 'Investing in socially responsible companies is a must for public pension funds–because there is no better alternative', *Journal of Business Ethics*, 56(2): 99–129.

Sevenhuijsen, S. (2003) *Citizenship and the Ethics of Care: Feminist Considerations on Justice, Morality and Politics*, London: Routledge.

Seyfang, G. (2003) 'Growing cohesive communities one favour at a time: social exclusion, active citizenship and time banks', *International Journal of Urban and Regional Research*, 27(3): 699–706.

Seyfang, G. (2006) 'Harnessing the potential of the social economy? Time banks and UK public policy', *International Journal of Sociology and Social Policy*, 26(9/10): 430–43.

Seyfang, G. and Smith, A. (2007) 'Grassroots innovations for sustainable development: towards a new research and policy agenda', *Environmental Politics*, 16(4): 584–603.

Shiva, V. (1991) *The Violence of Green Revolution: Third World Agriculture, Ecology and Politics*, London: Zed Books.

Singh, J. (2008) 'The UK Nanojury as upstream public engagement', *Participatory Learning and Action*, 58, 27–32. Available from: http://pubs.iied.org/pdfs/G02854.pdf [Accessed February 2020].

Smith, A. (1806) *An Inquiry into the Nature and Causes of the Wealth of Nations* [1776], (3rd edn), Edinburgh: William Creech.

Smith, A. (1812) *The Theory of Moral Sentiments* [1759], (11th edn), London: Cadell & Davies.

Solow, R.M. (1956) 'A contribution to the theory of economic growth', *The Quarterly Journal of Economics*, 70(1): 65–94.

Spivak, G.C. (1994) 'Can the subaltern speak?', in Williams, P. and Chrisman, L. (eds) *Colonial Discourse and Postcolonial Theory: A Reader*, New York: Columbia University Press, pp. 66–111.

Stiglitz, J. (2009) *Freefall: Free Markets and the Sinking of the Global Economy*, London: Penguin.

Stiglitz, J., Sen, A. and Fitoussi, J-P. (2010) *Report by the Commission on the Measurement of Economic Performance and Social Progress*. Paris: Commission on the Measurement of Economic Performance and Social Progress.

Stilgoe, J., Owen, R. and Macnaghten, P. (2013) 'A framework for responsible innovation', *Research Policy*, 42(9): 1568–80.

Stirling, A. (2008) '"Opening up" and "closing down": power, participation, and pluralism in the social appraisal of technology', *Science, Technology, & Human Values*, 33(2): 262–94.

Summers, L. (2013) 'Why Stagnation Might Prove to be the New Normal', *Financial Times*, 15 December. Available from: http://larrysummers.com/commentary/financial-times-columns/why-stagnation-might-prove-to-be-the-new-normal/ [Accessed August 2019].

Sutcliffe, H. (2011) *A Report on Responsible Research and Innovation for the European Commission*. Available from: http://ec.europa.eu/research/science-society/document_library/pdf_06/rri-report-hilary-sutcliffe_en.pdf [Accessed 19 December 2019].

Swan, T.W. (1956) 'Economic growth and capital accumulation', *Economic Record*, 32(2): 334–61.

Swann, G.M.P. (2009) *The Economics of Innovation*, Cheltenham: Edward Elgar.

Teo, T. (2010) 'What is epistemological violence in the empirical social sciences?' *Social and Personality Psychology Compass*, 4/5: 295–303.

Toynbee, A.J. (1953) *The World and the West*, Oxford: Oxford University Press.

Truman, H. (1964) *Public Papers of the Presidents of the United States: Harry S. Truman*, Washington, DC: US Government Printing Office.

Tucker, A.W. and Straffin Jr, P.D. (1983) 'The mathematics of Tucker: a sampler', *The Two-Year College Mathematics Journal*, 14(3): 228–32.

Tuhiwai-Smith, L. (2002) *Decolonizing Methodologies: Research and Indigenous Peoples*, London: Zed Books.

UN [United Nations] (2005) 'General Assembly Approves Declaration Banning All Forms of Cloning', *UN News*, 8 March. Available from: https://news.un.org/en/story/2005/03/131092-general-assembly-approves-declaration-banning-all-forms-cloning [Accessed January 2020].

US [United States Government] (2014) 'US Government Gain-of-Function Deliberative Process and Research Funding Pause on Selected Gain-of-Function Research Involving Influenza, MERS, and SARS Viruses'. Available from: www.phe.gov/s3/dualuse/Documents/gain-of-function.pdf [Accessed December 2019].

van de Poel, I. and Sand, M. (2018) 'Varieties of responsibility: two problems of responsible innovation', *Synthese*. Available from: https://rdcu.be/bZ4eh [Accessed December 2019].

van den Bergh, J.C.J.M. (2011) 'Environment versus growth – a criticism of "degrowth" and a plea for "a-growth"', *Ecological Economics*, 70(5): 881–90.

van Oudheusden, M. (2014) 'Where are the politics in responsible innovation? European governance, technology assessments, and beyond', *Journal of Responsible Innovation*, 1(1): 67–86.

Vasen, F. (2017) 'Responsible innovation in developing countries: an enlarged agenda', in L. Adveld, R. van Dam-Mieras, T. Swierstra, S. Lavrijssen, K. Linse and J. van den Hoven (eds) *Responsible Innovation 3: A European Agenda?*, Heidelberg: Springer International Publishing, pp 93–109.

Virki, T. (2007) 'Nokia's Cheap Phone Tops Electronics Chart', *Reuters*, 3 May. Available from: https://uk.reuters.com/article/us-nokia-history/nokias-cheap-phone-tops-electronics-chart-idUKL0262945620070503 [Accessed August 2019].

Visvanathan, S. (1988) 'On the Annals of the Laboratory State', in Nandy, A. (ed) *Science, Hegemony and Violence: A Requiem for Modernity*, Tokyo: United Nations University.

von Schomberg, R. (2011) 'Prospects for technology assessment in a framework of responsible research and innovation', in M. Dusseldorp and R. Beecroft (eds) *Technikfolgen abschätzen lehren: Bildungspotenziale transdisziplinärer Methoden*, Wiesbaden: Vs Verlag, pp 1–19.

von Schomberg, R. (2013) 'A vision of responsible innovation', in R. Owen, M. Heintz and J. Bessant (eds) *Responsible Innovation: Managing the Responsible Emergence of Science and Innovation in Society*, Chichester: John Wiley & Sons, pp 51–74.

Walsh, C. (2010) 'Development as Buen Vivir: institutional arrangements and (de)colonial entanglements', *Development*, 53(1): 15–21.

Wiedmann, T. and Minx, J. (2007) 'A definition of "carbon footprint"', in C.C. Pertsova (ed) *Ecological Economics Research Trends*, Hauppauge NY: Nova Science Publishers, pp 1–11.

Wilkinson, R. and Pickett, K. (2009) *The Spirit Level: Why Greater Equality Makes Societies Stronger*, London: Allen Lane.

Winner, L. (1993) 'Upon opening the black box and finding it empty: social constructivism and the philosophy of technology', *Science, Technology, & Human Values*, 18(3): 362–78.

World Bank (2008) *The Growth Report: Strategies for Sustained Growth and Inclusive Development*, Washington DC: World Bank.

Wright, C. and Nyberg, D. (2015) *Climate Change, Capitalism, and Corporations*, Cambridge: Cambridge University Press.

Zeschky, M., Widenmayer, B. and Gassmann, O. (2015) 'Frugal innovation in emerging markets', *Research Technology Management*, 54(4): 38–45.

Index

A

accountability
corporate 112, 113, 114, 116, 118–21
democratic 61,
in RI 63
public 56, 124
a-growth
approach to innovation 17, 19, 54, 72–3, 86, 90, 123, 133
in RS 76, 81, 136
paradigm 57
see also growth, agnostic
Alliance for Sustainable and Holistic Agriculture (ASHA) 107
anticipatory governance 31
appropriate technology 97

B

B Corps (certification) 121–23, 125, *see also* benefit corporation
B Lab 121
Barefoot College 82
Benefit Corporation 5, 56, 121
Buen Vivir 106–7

C

Cambridge Analytica 63
capital
accumulation 9
intangible 6, 112, 115–7, 119, 120
political 133
scalable 115, 118
social 41, 82, 87
spillover 115, 117–8, 119
sunk 115–6, 117, 118
synergy 118

capitalism 15–16, 59, 94, 95
failure of 100, 113
free-market 53, 129–30
care 130, 133–4
acting with 17, 55, 67, 141
as aspect of RS 90, 122, 137–9
commitment to 49, 55–6, 81, 102, 104–5, 107–9
ethics of 68–9, 72
for the future 8, 99, 102
governing with 69–70, 7, 104
in Global South 92, 105
Chernobyl 103
China 93, 106
climate change 108, 117, 139
as societal challenge 25, 28, 31, 132
responsibility for 35, 100, 113
co-production 89
Collingridge dilemma 63
Colombia 106
colonization 19, 92, 95
consequentialism 63, 72
Constructive Technology Assessment 31
corporate social responsibility (CSR) 31, 56, 78, 112–14

D

Daly, Herman 6, 12, 131
debt
crisis 84
holders 116
national 3, 49, 135
decision-making
and facts 28
and publics 19, 21, 29, 73, 79